CHRISTIAN SLATER
BACK FROM THE EDGE

CHRISTIAN SLATER
BACK FROM THE EDGE

NIGEL GOODALL

JOHN BLAKE

Published by John Blake Publishing Ltd,
3, Bramber Court, 2 Bramber Road,
London W14 9PB, England

www.blake.co.uk

First published in hardback in 2005

ISBN 1 84454 137 1

British Library Cataloguing-in-Publication Data:

A catalogue record for this book is available from the British Library.

Design by www.envydesign.co.uk

Printed in Great Britain by Creative Print and Design

1 3 5 7 9 10 8 6 4 2

Papers used by John Blake Publishing are natural, recyclable products
made from wood grown in sustainable forests. The manufacturing processes conform
to the environmental regulations of the country of origin.

Every attempt has been made to contact the relevant copyright-holders,
but some were unobtainable. We would be grateful if the appropriate people
could contact us.

To the memory of my mum and dad,
who never knew how important they were
in getting me this far.

Also by Nigel Goodall

What's Eating Johnny Depp

Kylie Naked: A Biography
(with Jenny Stanley-Clarke)

Demi Moore: The Most Powerful Woman in Hollywood

The Ultimate Queen
(with Peter Lewry)

Winona Ryder: The Biography

The Ultimate Cliff
(with Peter Lewry)

Jump Up: The Rise of the Rolling Stones

George Michael In His Own Words

The Complete Cliff Richard Chronicle
(with Peter Lewry)

Elton John: A Visual Documentary

Cher In Her Own Words

Cliff Richard: The Complete Recording Sessions
(with Peter Lewry)

www.nigelgoodall.co.uk

Acknowledgements

I t is no understatement to say that this book would not have been possible without the support of the following people. I would first of all like to thank my publisher, John Blake, for commissioning it; my editor, Mark Hanks, for later improving the manuscript with his excellent editing; and Graeme Andrew for the stunning cover and picture spreads. Thanks also to Keith Hayward, who did his usual 'researcher extraordinaire' bit in the UK, and, in New York, Jimmy Stingray, who spent countless hours following up my requests for information: Sean Delaney at the British Film Institute Library for all his wonderful help and guidance with film production notes, scripts and articles; John Tucker at the Professional Children's School in New York for confirming some factual information; and Mark Barker for helping me on filmography matters and tracking down some obscure sources. I would also like to thank Raymond

Jax, Tawd b Dorenfeld, Taliesyn Flaherty, Robert Liroff, Wendy Hunter and Chris Samson for sharing with me their memories of the stage-play version of *Heathers* in 1990s Petaluma, northern California; Charlotte Rasmussen for all the support in the world; and my dearest friend Anne Sprinks for getting me through it – you are a truly beautiful and amazing woman.

In addition, two books *Robin Hood: Prince of Thieves: The Official Movie Book* by Garth Pearce (Hamlyn, 1991) and *Winona Ryder* by Dave Thompson (Taylor, 1997) provided some valuable information.

Contents

Chapter 1

No Straitjacket Required

Saturday, 22 January 2005 was Christian Slater's last night as Randle P McMurphy. It was the night that followed a supposed (and later denied) knife attack on Christian outside the stage door and was a typically cold winter's day in London. Although by evening the temperature had dropped below zero, the chill didn't stop anyone from turning out to see Christian's final performance in *One Flew Over the Cuckoo's Nest* at the Gielgud Theatre in the heart of London's West End.

Looking around the audience that night, one could not help but wonder if there wasn't anyone that didn't leave the theatre angered and indignant – not at Christian's performance, but at the barbarity of the treatment inflicted on the role that Christian had been playing for the previous six months, the one that made Jack Nicholson so famous (or the one that Nicholson had been made famous by) and the one that would forever cause Christian to be constantly compared to the veteran Hollywood actor. As *Daily Telegraph* theatre critic Dominic Cavendish noted, if anyone should fall into the trap of reassuring themselves that what happens to Christian's character and those of his fellow inmates of a psychiatric ward doesn't happen any more, they should think again: 'The most shocking thing about Dale Wasserman's adaptation of Ken Kesey's novel is that it can be held up as a play for today; the old asylums have been shut down in the drive towards care in the community, but, in certain key respects, what went on back then goes on now.'

Although Cavendish admits that his comment sounded wildly sensationalist, it was nevertheless, he discovered, a conclusion easily drawn from readily available sources of information. And although he admitted he was a theatre reviewer and not a health correspondent, when he went online to gain a greater understanding of the procedures referred to in the play, and to see whether the abuses described (based on Kesey's own experience of working on psychiatric wards in the late 1950s) could be corroborated by published testimonies, he didn't expect to find present-day parallels. 'Call me naïve,' he wrote, 'but because *Cuckoo's Nest* is so fixed in the mind through its 1975 film incarnation, I'd assumed it was a museum piece.'

He couldn't be more wrong. Yes, he knew that psychiatric medicine was big business, from the early sequence in the film and the same scene in the play, when patients are seen queuing up for their daily doses of medicines, presenting an image that, according to Cavendish, is more pertinent today than ever; a quarter of drugs prescribed by the NHS in

2

Britain every year are for mental-health problems, and the amount spent on anti-depressants has soared. In the States, George W Bush has declared war on mental illness, proclaiming, 'Mental disability is not a scandal; it is an illness. And, like physical illness, it is treatable, especially when the treatment comes early.'

As Cavendish also noted in his programme notes, 'For the foreseeable future, Americans will – like Britons – keep taking the pills. That in itself is concerning, but it's what else that's on offer for those in need of treatment that foments nightmares. The dreaded lobotomy, the final weapon in character Nurse Ratched's armoury, enabling her to deal with recalcitrant patients, has long been discredited, its reputation indelibly associated with heartbreaking stories of patients left brain-damaged, among them, most famously, Tennessee Williams's sister Rose, John Kennedy's sister Rosemary and the Hollywood actress Frances Farmer.'

Once seen as a simple, cheap solution to a wide range of disorders, from acute anxiety to chronic backache, the pre-frontal lobotomy is nowadays regarded as an abomination, and the awarding of the 1949 Nobel Prize to one of its pioneers, Egas Moniz, remains a source of bitter contention. Nevertheless, continued Cavendish, 'Psychosurgery or neurosurgical treatment on the frontal lobes of the brain continues to this day. The techniques have been refined and the number of people treated is negligible by comparison with the 50,000 estimated to have been lobotomised in America between the 1930s and the late 1950s. But it goes on.'

In England and Wales between 1997 and 1999, seventeen psychosurgery operations were authorised, a number that dwindled to nine between 1999 and 2001. Even so, that was still nine too many as far as Mind, the UK's National Association for Mental Health, was concerned. The charity stated, 'Mind is not happy with the continued use of psychosurgery and believes that there should be a rigorous review to determine whether any continued use is justified.'

In 2003, in an article entitled 'New Surgery To Control Behaviour', the *LA Times* reported, 'At several institutions around the world, including hospitals affiliated with Harvard and Brown universities' medical schools, surgeons have been operating on dozen of patients each year with severe psychiatric problems, including depression and, more commonly, obsessive-compulsive disorder.'

If the numbers of 'psychosurgery' patients remain small, but significant, what of electric-shock treatment, such a favourite of the *Cuckoo's Nest* staff, asked Cavendish. 'An astonishing number of people continue to be given electro-convulsive therapy (ECT), even though the medical community remains divided about its benefits. And all too often those electrodes are applied without proper consent. In Italy, where it began more than sixty-two years ago, ECT has almost been abolished, but in the UK thousands are estimated to receive ECT every year: 9,000 in England alone in 2002. And in the US, the figure rises to 100,000 a year.'

In 2001, Mind conducted a survey of ECT patients and found that almost three-quarters of respondents weren't given any information about possible side-effects, and that over half of them claimed to be unaware that they could refuse treatment. In total, some 84 per cent of respondents reported that they experienced side-effects after receiving treatment, including short- and long-term memory loss, an inability to concentrate, headaches, drowsiness and confusion.

The internet is awash with testimonies of people who feel that their lives have been scarred by ECT. 'The biggest medical mistake of my life,' an American woman called Faith declares on a site called etc.org, while David, a British respondent, sums up his experience thus: 'I was tortured and left damaged.'

Perhaps this is what still makes *Cuckoo's Nest* as relevant today as it was when it was first published. Kesey presents the tale of a man who takes on the authorities at a psychiatric institution and briefly manages to drive them nuts, and in doing so he inspires the inmates around him to stick up for themselves. And perhaps the film resonates so much today because part of the tragedy of the play and film comes from knowing that there are no McMurphys to call on for those who get caught up in the mental-health system. Hospitalisation and *de facto* incarceration might be much rarer today than they were thirty years ago, but the feelings of powerlessness experienced by individuals classified as mentally ill are as potent as ever. Beginning as a tale of spirited rebellion, *Cuckoo's Nest* becomes a bleak reminder about the potential for those within the medical establishment to abuse their authority and treat their patients as second-class citizens.

Maybe Cavendish was right, and maybe this was the reason why Christian took on the role. But maybe also it is that the wild, fun-loving radical character of McMurphy, incarcerated for engaging in sexual relations with a minor, is a role that every actor dreams of playing. To avoid prison work,

McMurphy feigns madness and is sent to a mental asylum, where his fellow patients are sad, over-sedated and institutionalised. McMurphy promptly plans to inject colour, life and laughter into their grey world of strict rules and regulations. His only obstacle is Nurse Ratched, an infallibly cool and immaculate air-hostess figure, all flicked hair and lipstick, who cares for her 'boys' with a possessive motherly love. Into her regimented ward, McMurphy introduces the chaos of gambling, indoor basketball, democratic voting rights and glamorous visitors, instigating a vicious duel of words between the two. Each plays their own psychological game to outwit the other, but soon Ratched's demeanour begins to crack, revealing a cruel, sadistic streak.

Published in 1962 to immediate popular and critical acclaim, *One Flew Over the Cuckoo's Nest* is a grim political satire that explores themes of individuality and rebellion against conformity, as well as ideas that were widely discussed at the time when the US was committed to opposing Communism and totalitarian regimes. The 1975 film with Nicholson won five Academy Awards, and the movie became a cult classic. Less familiar was the original play on Broadway a decade earlier, starring Kirk Douglas in the role that Christian took on, which became a highlight of the 2004 Edinburgh Festival. As one Festival reviewer noted, forty years on, the timing couldn't have been better for a revived stage version. However, there were some cynics who saw it as nothing more than an attempt by Christian to revive a flagging film career and to rise above accusations voiced by many that he was a washed-up movie star.

If Slater had indeed taken on the role to scotch the rumours touted by cynics, the job was well done. Even though, as critic Vivien Devlin noted, the production had a minimalist set featuring a grey-painted day room with nursing station and swing doors, combined with authentic costume design comprising hospital pyjamas and period clothes, 'Slater's McMurphy comes over as a cheeky, law-breaking rebel, inspired perhaps by Kesey's true-life drug-induced Merry Pranksters. The play has an ensemble of comic actors and comedians who play the inmates and staff with meticulous detail to physical mannerism and character.' Similar praise went to 'the chalk-white, skinny, wide-eyed McKenzie Crook', as Devlin described him, lauding him as being 'utterly convincing as poor stuttering, terrified friend Billy'. Devlin then went on to heap praise on the production of the play: 'Finely directed with a perfect sense of pace and tension, the dramatic thrust of this very intimate play moves from moment of manic energy to such heartbreaking pathos it makes you weep. Once again, five Oscars. This is a masterpiece.'

Masterpiece or not, the staging of the production was not without its difficulties. Not long after director Guy Masterson suddenly quit, Christian went down with a case of chicken pox and then, two weeks later, was diagnosed with a secondary infection that threatened the show's continued running. But on the day of the opening performance, at Edinburgh's Assembly Rooms on 6 August 2004, and after less than two hours of full cast rehearsals in ten days, producer Nica Burns had nothing but praise for him: 'He's one of the most heroic actors that I've ever met. He's hardly seen the set tonight and he doesn't even know where the doors are, let alone the chairs. Tonight, we're jumping off a cliff.'

Not that anyone would have noticed. The audience reviews, let alone the critics, were overwhelmingly favourable. And, although the Assembly Rooms' director, Bill Burdett-Coutts, was slightly worried at the very start, because 'Christian went very pale for a public dress rehearsal, there were no flaws. It was remarkable. It was brilliant.'

Less than brilliant, however, was one of the backstage dramas that had been going on behind the scenes before the production transferred to London in September. By then, Terry Johnson had stepped in to replace director Guy Masterson, who had quit, complaining of stress, personal problems and king-sized egos. And the word circulating through the theatre grapevine was that it was the fact that he could not develop a happy working relationship with Christian that had tipped him over the edge. Making matters worse were reports from the first rehearsals, prior to Christian's health setbacks, most of which described Christian's strong temperament.

Not that Frances Barber, who played Nurse Ratched, would agree, despite admitting, '[At first] I thought, Oh, here we go. We're going to have a Hollywood arsehole. But he's not. He's absolutely fantastic in every way. He's like my little brother, although he would probably say I'm like his mother. He's one of the greatest actors I've worked with, and he's one of the nicest men.'

But perhaps it is a matter of perspective? If it was true that the failure to develop an easy working relationship between Slater and Masterson contributed to Masterson's departure, then it wasn't the first time that Christian had been identified as a force to be reckoned with. In 1998, for instance, he told reporters, 'I like to be loud. I like to break things. I like to have a good time. I have that side to me, and, if I can express it in a creative manner, we're all a lot safer.'

More tellingly, that same year he admitted, 'There was a part of me that felt I had more to contribute than I really did. I would get involved with projects where there were people with less experience than me so that I could come in and feel superior.' But, if you asked him if he was still doing that, he would say no. And, although he thought Masterson was a lovely man and very creative, such praise wasn't unqualified: 'He had some things going on personally that made it difficult for him.'

It had been Masterson who, on the strength of his success with *Twelve Angry Men* during the previous year's Fringe Festival, had chosen *Cuckoo's Nest* as the ideal follow-up, with Christian – urged on by his mother, Mary Jo Slater – as its star. 'If ever an actor was born to play this role, it is Christian Slater,' he told Ed McCraken of Scotland's *Sunday Herald*. 'He's thirty-five years old, which is the age of the character. He's Californian, and the character is Californian. He is perfect for it, and, believe me, he is utterly amazing.'

All the same, Christian was nervous at first – or at least that's what he told journalist Aidan Smith during pre-Fringe rehearsals at the then vacant Duchess Theatre in London during a sultry summer afternoon. 'I've had a lot of Jack Nicholson comparisons in my career, and he was phenomenal in the movie, but my mother told me I had to come to Edinburgh because it's such a special place.'

But perhaps more than the place, it was Christian's chequered past that attracted Masterson to have him in the play. 'The personal history came from his edge. He wouldn't have been so edgy if he wasn't a troubled character. I've met Hollywood actors all my life. You grow up in Hollywood, as a child star in the public eye, and the pressures are just beyond anything that we comprehend. You couple that with an anarchic personality and, yeah, you're going to do some troubling things.'

In his interview with Aidan Smith, Christian affirmed that he was 'trying to remain focused and energetic and positive and concentrating on my acting, being a good man and living kind of quieter than before', although his interpretation of the term 'quieter' was a little more broad than most people's. On the evening of the day that he spoke with Smith, he was reportedly asked to leave London's Stringfellow's nightspot for refusing to remove his Richard Nixon mask.

It was Christian's late-'90s descent into rehab, coupled with his descent from being a bankable A-list star, that most of all intrigued the director, who put it down to simply a series of 'terrible films and bad advice'. To paraphrase Gloria Swanson in *Sunset Boulevard*, all through Christian's cinematic dip, he remained big; it was the pictures that got small. 'I never thought of his star dimming,' said Masterson. 'You can see his ability in it. [He just made] bad choices in films. I actually enjoyed him in *Hard Rain*, which was a bit of a shit thriller, but he was superb in it.

'Anthony Hopkins was going down that route of drinking and being dangerous, and he made a choice that changed his life: he went back on stage and then went into this psychological thriller called *Silence of the Lambs*. Now he is regarded as one of the leading actors in the world.'

As Ed McCraken noted in his *Sunday Herald* feature, however, for every Hopkins who has resuscitated his or her career on stage, there is a Keanu Reeves playing *Hamlet* to clamorous boos. Frances Barber was also painfully aware that, for Christian, treading the boards was like treading on eggshells. 'Let's face it, he's got more to lose than anybody in this. He's the Hollywood superstar, not us. He's playing McMurphy. I mean, Nurse Ratched is a great iconic part, but he's got more to lose than me and, hopefully, has much to gain.'

As if exorcising critical demons, taking on a role made famous by the man to whom Christian has constantly been compared was indeed a risk, capable of being seen as either wanton self-destruction or a stroke of brave genius. As it happened, it turned out to be the latter. 'Christian is very realistic about [the comparisons that people will strike],' recounted Masterson just days before the production would play its first performance, 'but he's not scared. He's going to deliver a performance that will defy the critics. They're going to come in saying, "He's not Jack Nicholson" and go out saying, "No, he's not Jack Nicholson; he's Christian Slater."'

Chapter 2

New York, New York

Greenwich Village in New York is probably one of the most exciting places on Earth. For over 100 years, the small area located below Fourteenth Street and west of Broadway has been a Mecca to the creative, rebellious and bohemian.

Michael Hawkins and Mary Jo Slater were living in Greenwich Village during the summer of 1969 when their first child was born. Although they could never have been described as conventional parents, nor was the world in which they circulated conventional. Mary Jo, in her early twenties, was an agent's assistant, and Michael a struggling actor who was by then, in Mary Jo's words, 'a renowned performer, playing Shakespeare and the classics on Broadway, and even starring with the Royal Shakespeare Company'. He had also made a number of undistinguished appearances in such quickly forgotten flicks as *Torture Garden* and *They Came From Beyond Space.*

Born Tom Slater in Shaker Heights, Ohio, Michael was raised in Texas and Tennessee, where his father worked in textile manufacturing. The two men never saw eye to eye. 'A few years after his death, I even changed my name to emphasise the difference between us,' says Michael. 'I think the big problem was that we never had any interests in common at all. I was a complete mystery to him.'

Michael met Mary Jo backstage in 1967 at a Greenwich Village production of the anti-Vietnam satire *MacBird*, in which Michael was playing a supporting role to the then emergent Stacey Keach in the lead part. A native New Yorker from Trenton, New Jersey, Mary Jo, at the time of attending the play, was due to graduate the following year from the American Academy of Dramatic Arts, where she was studying drama to be an actor alongside one of her best friends, Danny de Vito. However, she admits that she just knew she 'wasn't going to be one of those folks who did really well'.

Suitably impressed with Michael's onstage performance, she announced to her friends in the intermission that she was 'going to marry that guy', and after the curtain came down she went backstage and got an introduction out of her companion for that evening, another former classmate, Cleavon Little. Michael was equally taken aback. 'When a woman makes it clear that she's interested in you, how can you not hit it off?' Eight months later, they were married, and a year after that, on 18 August 1969 – the same day that Woodstock saw out the end of an era – their first child was born: Christian Michael Leonard, named after Marlon Brando's character of *Bounty* mutineer Fletcher Christian. The proud parents even pinned a notice to his birth certificate announcing that 'there was no one greater'.

As well as being the year in which Christian arrived into the world, 1969 was also the year in which Richard Nixon was inaugurated as the thirty-seventh President of the United States, continuing the war in Vietnam; the Stonewall riot in New York City marked the beginning of the gay-rights movement; the Apollo 11 astronauts took their first steps on the moon; Senator Edward Kennedy pleaded guilty to leaving the scene of a fatal accident at Chappaquiddick, Massachusetts; and, just eighteen days before Christian was born, Elvis Presley stepped out on to a Las Vegas stage for the first of his history-making public appearances after an eight-year hiatus.

If it's true that Christian spent most of his childhood surrounded by either theatre, film or television people, then, with such an upbringing, it should not be that surprising that a thespian future seemed destined from the start. Perhaps nowhere is that better expressed than in the fact that, when he was only three months old, Mary Jo carried him out on to the stage of an empty theatre and showed him the view out into the auditorium where an audience would normally be seated and told him, 'This is your life, my son.'

Early in the 1970s, when Christian was still an infant, Mary Jo, having spent several years as an agent, decided she wanted to produce shows. And, as luck would have it, her gynaecologist was married to an actress who at the time was in the same soap opera as Michael. And, again, as luck would have it, he was the same gynaecologist who looked after the wife of Manny Azenberg, the almost legendary producer of all Neil Simon's plays in America. Literally via word of mouth, thinking how it would serve as a step up the production ladder, Mary Jo settled for a job as Azenberg's office receptionist, but, to her surprise, despite previously working as an agent in her own right, she still had to start her new job working the telephones. 'I was not used to answering phones myself,' she confessed, and so she did the next best thing: she opted to produce an off-Broadway play of her own, which of course 'pissed everyone off' in the process.

Starting Here, Starting Now was a production whose title song, interestingly enough, was recorded by a young and relatively unknown singer named Barbra Streisand. And, as if that wasn't enough, the first-night party was held in Francis Ford Coppola's suite at the Sherry–Netherland, and another relative unknown, Robert Redford, did the TV commercial for the production.

Back at Azenberg's office, however, Mary Jo still couldn't answer the phones fast enough. In the end, when she put Neil Simon on hold indefinitely and almost forgot he was hanging on, she was fired for being the worst receptionist the office had ever had. It's therefore a little surprising that, on the same day she got fired, she was asked if she would like to cast Simon's new play, *Chapter Two*, on Broadway. Mary Jo, of course, accepted, and the play was so successful that it was turned into a Hollywood movie in 1979, starring James Caan, and suddenly Mary Jo was a fully fledged casting director. 'I love it passionately,' she says. 'Casting can make or break a movie or a show, but the real secret is passion. If you don't love what you're doing, don't do it. That applies to everything in life.'

Her responsibilities as a casting director meant that she could also take Christian with her to work. 'He grew up backstage and in auditions,' she remembers. 'I would be casting Broadway shows and he would sit there, wide-eyed.'

At other times, he would go along to work with Michael. 'I remember hanging out backstage at my father's shows and loving the make-believe,' Christian recalls. 'I'd bring my action figures and play with them. There were lots of places to hide and I'd sneak around, spying on the girls as they were getting dressed.' Whether he was doing theatre or Broadway shows, 'it looked like so much fun that I really knew that I wanted to be part of that from an early age'.

The earliest Christian became part of 'that' was in 1976, when he was seven and, almost ironically, Michael and Mary Jo got divorced – although, by the end, Christian confides, their marriage was 'a total and complete disaster'. Christian's first appearance on national television in a daytime soap opera was on *One Life To Live*. Everybody applauded his performance, and that was it: he was completely sold on the idea. At the same time, however, he was also facing the difficulty of having his parents go their separate ways. Like any seven-year-old in the same position, he felt that there was little he could do. 'There's so much anger there, and there wasn't a lot of maturity going on. There wasn't a lot of sanity going on either, but I did the best I could.'

Two years before that, one of Christian's fondest memories of growing up in New York had been watching his father on television. On one occasion, Michael, who was starring in

ABC's *Ryan's Hope* (in which, interestingly enough, Christian himself would later play a role), had an important scene. 'My father's head was stuck in an oven and he was dying,' remembers Christian. 'I couldn't figure out what was happening, and I started flipping out.' Later, after Michael explained it, Christian was hooked – and not for the last time – on the business of make-believe, surely what acting is all about: making the unbelievable believable. It was probably what attracted Christian to the idea of becoming an actor in the first place.

But, sadly, in the years that followed, a feud developed between father and son – or did it? The idea that there had been a fallout came about when an American movie magazine ran a story that Christian's mother was seemingly taking a lot of credit for her son's success, also claiming that Christian agreed. An apparently angered father then wrote a letter to the magazine that ran, 'I take full credit for Christian's success. I have made him a star. Someday, no doubt when I'm dead, maybe Christian will give me the credit I deserve and crave.'

In other quarters, things weren't as bad as they seemed. Indeed, rumours on the Hollywood grapevine seemed to suggest entirely the opposite when it was reported that Christian often speaks most warmly of his father, as a roguish, almost Byronic figure, despite Mary Jo's 1989 appraisal that Michael is 'not an intellectual by any stretch of the imagination'.

According to *People Weekly* in 1993, however, Christian's relationship with his father hadn't altogether improved; even though they were both living in Los Angeles, the two rarely spoke, which Christian apparently still finds upsetting. 'I think he needs to be acknowledged by me that he's my father and had something to do with my life, which I'm willing to do,' he says. 'But, for him, that's not enough, and that's unfair. Nobody deserves full credit for anybody's success. I have to hold true to myself.'

All the same, Christian continued to make the best out of a helpless situation, which meant arriving at school each day and fitting in as best he knew how. New York City's Dalton School was an independent, co-educational day school that to this day is recognised for its rigorous, innovative educational curriculum offering its 1,300 students a breadth of stimulating and challenging programmes taught by a dedicated, professional faculty. Although he might have been in class most days, most of his after-school hours were spent doing his homework on the set of a movie or TV show, wherever Mary Jo was working.

Not that Christian was concerned. 'I was raised by my mother, who's grown to become my greatest confidante and the person I trust most,' he revealed. 'But she got married young, and, when she and my father split, I think things were very difficult for her. So I think I gravitated towards father-figure types I met in the theatre – and, let me tell you, some of them were pretty confused individuals.'

Christian met one of those father-figure types while Mary Jo was still working on *One Life to Live*. One day, Christian remembers, a day player came over to give him a helping hand with his homework. His name was Dan Lauria, a former 'Big Brother of the Year', and probably best known as the father on US TV's *The Wonder Years*. From the first time they met, Lauria remained a constant presence in Christian's life. Indeed, Lauria recalls that Christian was 'as close to a son as I'll ever have'. At the time, Lauria was running a theatre across the street from the Slaters' apartment, 'so Christian was always in the theatre – painting sets, cleaning toilets and acting. He's a real theatre person. Most people don't realise that. I always thought Christian was happier onstage than anywhere else, even in real life.'

Christian himself would probably agree with that summation. 'I don't think of myself as offbeat and weird,' he once said of himself. 'As a kid, I saw myself as the type of guy who would run into a building to save the baby.' However, this attitude seems to be at odds with his later confession that he was 'a shy, quiet kid who was happiest playing by myself with my toys rather than hanging around other people. But then showbiz happened and that opened me up a bit and I made the choice to act on my own.'

That choice really came two years later, when Mary Jo was working on *The Joe Franklin Show*. 'I was this nine-year-old little boy, watching from the sidelines,' recalled Christian. 'Joe Franklin looked over and saw me, and asked me to come on, so I sat down. And I guess that night, Michael Kidd, the director – who was doing *The Music Man* at the time – saw it and asked me to come in and audition. I sang "Zip A Dee Doo Dah" and got the job!' Signed to play the cute, all-American character of Winthrop opposite Dick Van Dyke in the show, he was also given a couple of solo songs to perform in the show. 'I did "Gary, Indiana" and "Wells–Fargo Wagon", although I can barely remember them now.' But one thing Christian did remember was that, 'In the beginning, I'd be on stage and start waving to my mother in the audience. I was just a young kid. Then, as the show went on, I began to understand what it was all about. We toured for nine months and it drilled into my head that I was going to do this or die. There was no escape. I was lucky; I was never a child star. Instead, I gained a lot of professional experience and learned how to deal with people.'

For Mary Jo, however, the beginning of the national tour across America wasn't quite as simple to explain away. 'I put my baby on a bus and said goodbye,' she recalled. 'I felt terrible. I thought he would get showbusiness out of his system. Wrong. He loved every second of it.' At the same time, though, and like so many other child actors before and since, Christian found the end of a production jarring; the closing performance of *The Music Man* was, according to Mary Jo, 'so emotional. They were his family for nine months. Even when some reporter stuck a mic in his face, he said, "I can't talk now because I am about to cry."'

With the success of *The Music Man* behind him, and after he had said his goodbyes to the rest of the cast, Christian went back to school and enrolled into New York's Professional Children's School, where, he recalled, 'I had blonde spiky hair, and I wore a snakeskin jacket and glasses that wrapped around my face.'

If Mary Jo's idea was to put her son's acting career on hold until the next vacation, things didn't go exactly according to plan; school records indicate that Christian entered the sixth grade during the autumn of 1981 and withdrew at the end of the ninth grade in the spring of 1984. By this time, although by all accounts a popular student, at the age of fifteen he was working almost full-time in Hollywood, so it was no surprise to anyone that he wasn't actually spending that much time attending classes. After spending the lion's share of his time during that period making four or five movies, it made sense for him to move out to California permanently, which he did.

The school itself, however, has a unique and interesting history that also gives a remarkable insight into the development, care and education of child actors from which people like Christian would eventually benefit. The concept for a school especially for young performers dates back to October 1913, when Jane Harris Hall and Jean Greer Robinson attended a Broadway performance of *Daddy Long Legs*. After the show, while making their way backstage, the two women happened upon several of the children from the cast playing cards. On striking up a conversation with the youngsters, they learned that the children didn't attend school and that they could barely read and write.

Upon later investigation, Hall and Robinson discovered that public and private schools couldn't or wouldn't accommodate the schedules of stage children and that most children working on the stage were simply skipping school. Seeing the need to provide adequate education, they decided to establish a school designed especially for New York's stage or professional children. Both ladies were already deeply involved in efforts to improve the lot of New York's actors and actresses, and together they had founded the Rehearsal Club, a non-profit residential club for young actresses.

The school admitted its first students on 6 January 1914 in rented space at the Rehearsal Club. From the start, the school's approach was to give the child of the stage and screen an opportunity to obtain a thorough education and at the same time permit the young actor or actress to continue with his or her profession, while still being flexible with its hours to enable rehearsals and manager's appointments and the various interruptions demanded by a life on the stage. At the same time, the school would insist upon and achieve a very high standard of scholarship. Within a year, the school was enrolling over 100 students.

One of the most attractive aspects of the school, then and now, was that it strove to adapt to the children, rather than the other way around. Usually, the school day would begin at ten o'clock in the morning and finish promptly at two in the afternoon. The idea was that those students who had professional engagements to keep could then miss class while a 'correspondence programme' would allow those working in touring shows to keep up with their school work while away. In other areas, the curriculum concentrated on maximising students' time while meeting state requirements for graduation, as most students and parents at that time considered high-school graduation the conclusion of their formal academic education.

Over time, changes in the entertainment industry were reflected in the student body. The silent-movie actors moved to California while radio began to be broadcast live from New York City. Vaudeville died, but Broadway entered the period of its greatest creativity, with child actors featuring prominently in dozens of productions. A few classical musicians and ballet dancers joined the ranks, but the mission of the school remained remarkably true to its original inspiration.

After the Second World War, there was an increased emphasis on academia, and the school launched its first major fundraising campaign to expand and improve its facilities in 1948. The number of faculty increased and, by 1956, fifty-five per cent of the school's graduates were attending college immediately upon graduation. Still occupying rented space (three floors in a commercial building on Broadway and 61st Street), in 1956 the school was able to purchase the building it currently occupies, which allowed space for additional classrooms, a physical-education programme and a proper cafeteria. All of these facilities were located directly across the street from the then proposed Lincoln Center complex, which over the next decade had a major impact on the school, serving as the primary reason why, through the '70s and '80s, the numbers of classical musicians and ballet dancers attending the school increased.

Although the school seemed the perfect place for Christian to meet others with the same interest in acting and performing, his attendance there didn't really work because, during the period that he should have been in class, he was often away filming.

Christian had already had a small role in *Living Proof: The Hank Williams Jr Story*, starring Richard Thomas as the country singer. He then had a much bigger role in *The Legend of Billie Jean*, starring opposite Keith Jordan and Helen Slater, who Christian had a crush on, although this failed to develop into anything more than that, despite the fact that, as Christian jokes, 'we share the same surname'.

Fresh from her breakthrough title role in *Supergirl*, Helen was chosen for the role of Billie Jean from an audition call of

over 100 other actresses, all reading for the same part. It was
a character Helen loved at first sight. 'She's a very free spirit,
full of unfocused energy,' she enthused. 'I think kids in
America are going though a crisis now because they don't
have any dreams any more; they don't have something they
want to be. Billie Jean starts out having no real passion, no
dream, and then she finds something she really believes in
and fights for it.'

The Legend of Billie Jean told the story of pretty teen Billie
Jean Davy, who, with her father dead and her mother busy
trying to land a steady beau, spent her time with her brother,
Binx (played by Christian), riding his moped and dreaming
of life in Vermont, several climate zones away from the
humid, omnipresent heat of their Texas town.

One day, on their way from their trailer-park home to a
swimming hole, the Davy kids run afoul of rich boy Hubie
Pyatt and his cronies, who steal and later trash the scooter
Binx bought with his father's paltry life-insurance benefits.
Demanding payment from Hubie and his merchant dad for
the damage that's been inflicted on both the bike and her
brother's face, Billie Jean narrowly escapes being raped by the
elder Pyatt. In the ensuing scuffle, Binx accidentally shoots
Pyatt, sending himself, Billie Jean and their friends, Ophelia
and Putter, on the lam. When the 'Billie Jean Gang' becomes
a media sensation, Pyatt capitalises on their notoriety by
selling T-shirts and bric-a-brac, while policeman Ringwald,
who feels guilty for having refused to help Billie Jean, tries
to bring in the kids without anyone getting hurt. However,
when the gang mock-kidnaps rich amateur film-maker
Lloyd, unaware that he's the district attorney's son, the

situation spins out of control. Soon, Lloyd's videotape of the suddenly crop-topped, Joan of Arc-emulating, eminently telegenic Billie Jean elevates a local headline into a national sensation, and even Lloyd's attraction to Billie Jean can't protect her from becoming a media lightning rod.

Even though the film didn't do very well at the box office, it did give Christian the experience he would need for what was to follow. What is perhaps strangely interesting is that, while not a box-office smash by any means, *The Legend of Billie Jean* still ended up earning almost double the gross of what Christian's breakthrough movie would make five years later.

Chapter 3

First Movies

Shortly after completing *The Legend of Billie Jean*, Christian left for Italy to start work on Jean-Jacques Annaud's ambitious adaptation of Umberto Eco's acclaimed novel *The Name of the Rose*, a spellbinding tale of death and intrigue set within the confines of a fourteenth-century cloister.

Eco's novel, first published in Italy in 1980 and in America three years later, had sold four million copies worldwide, been translated into twenty-four languages and won numerous literary awards. The paperback rights were sold in the United States for $550,000, the highest figure ever paid for a translated work.

Director Jean-Jacques Annaud first discovered the novel in 1982 while promoting his previous year's *Quest for Life* in the Caribbean. During his stay there he read an article on the literary page of *Le Monde* about a book about to be published in France, a detective story set in a fourteenth-century monastery. 'I called up a friend in France to contact the publishing company, get a galley of the book and read it for me. He called back two days later and said, "I won't tell you any more, but come back earlier." I shortened my trip, went home and started reading. On page 200, I called my agent and said, "Get me the rights." On page 350, he called back and said, "The rights are gone. They're with RAI TV in Italy." On page 400, I phoned him and said, "Get me a meeting with Umberto Eco and one with RAI." By page 450, the meetings were arranged. And so began my passionate quest to film *The Name of the Rose.*'

The challenge, continues Annaud, 'was to make a two-hour film out of a 500-page book, with the complexity of having to entertain a worldwide audience and yet be something special. I've always had the ambition to get the two together. [I thought that] this may be the only opportunity in my life to have both elements of what I think a film should contain.'

According to the description in the book's cover blurb, *The Name of the Rose* is 'set in Italy in the Middle Ages and is not only a narrative of a murder investigation in a monastery in 1327, but also a chronicle of the fourteenth-century religious wars, a history of monastic orders, and a compendium of heretical movements'. Even the synopsis read much the same as the film turned out: 'One after the other, half a dozen monks are found murdered in the most bizarre of ways. A learned Franciscan who is sent to solve the mysteries finds himself involved in the frightening events.'

Although the film to some was considered a flop and in

other quarters quite preposterous, it was nevertheless the film that gave Christian his breakthrough role and, in the process, won him some rave notices. Perhaps interestingly, the film made less money at the box office than *Heathers* would three years later, which in itself seems strange when one considers that everyone still thinks of *Heathers* as the film that established Christian as a fully fledged star.

On the other hand, Christian is hardly mentioned in the production notes of *The Name of the Rose*. In fact, the casting process began with a very simple idea that only actors who were right for the part would be cast. If those actors happened to be stars, then fine, and, if they were complete unknowns, then, again, fine. It is in this respect that Christian is mentioned only briefly as a 'young New Yorker' but little else.

However, perhaps Christian was surprised that he even got a part. When *Premiere* magazine caught up with him for an interview in April 1989, two years after he had met Kim Walker, whom he was now dating and with whom he was about to co-star in *Heathers*, he was still astonished that he even got the part in the earlier movie: 'When I first read the script I thought, There's no way I can play a medieval monk; there's just no chance. It was such an intense role, with this wild love scene, and I was just sixteen. I was surprised Jean-Jacques Annaud cast me. I played Sean Connery's apprentice in the film, and our relationship on screen reflects real life: he was teaching me, and I was trying to take it all in.'

It was equally surprising, perhaps, that Annaud didn't seem that concerned that Connery, Christian and the other co-stars had contrasting accents. His attitude was, as long as they spoke English, why worry? Far more important to Annaud was the film's moody, Rembrandt-esque look and Christian's big-screen deflowering at the hands of the voluptuous Chilean actress Valentina Vargas, an act that, according to film critic James Cameron-Wilson, 'was one of the most unexpectedly erotic moments of 1980s cinema'. Even though Christian and Vargas became an item off screen as well as on, their relationship didn't last, possibly due to the age difference (he was, after all, only sixteen years old, while she was twenty-two).

Like the book, the cinema version of *The Name of the Rose* is set in a remote abbey in the north of Italy in 1327. Brother William of Baskerville, played by Sean Connery, is a studious and respected monk who arrives on horseback with his novice, played by Christian. Once inside the grounds, they are welcomed by the Abbot (Michael Lonsdale), who informs them of an unfortunate incident involving the death of one of their own, found broken and mutilated near the graveyard. They are told of a widespread belief that evil is at work in the abbey and, when elder monks surmise that the Devil himself roams the grounds, the inquisitive Brother William sets out to confirm this as unsound. When more bodies are discovered, however, hysteria breaks out, superstition running rife among the flock.

Brother William proceeds to piece together the fragments of evidence and then confronts the abbot with the information he discovers. It seems that hidden messages, found written in lemon juice on parchment, reveal details concerning a book that can kill and for which men would kill. The literature contains dangerous writings, the holy code of sorrow must prevail and a certain corruption in the form of comic images is forbidden and must be eradicated at all cost. The Bishop, however, is not convinced and a holy inquisition is called, led by Bernardo Gui (F Murray Abraham), a sadistic and unforgiving witch-hunter. On their arrival, they almost immediately accuse a young peasant girl, whose poverty-stricken quarters contain traces of witchcraft, if only in the form of a black cat and cockerel, which is nevertheless enough for the inquisition, who believe they have sought out the cloven-hoofed antichrist.

Also accused is Salvatore (Ron Perlman) – a deformed, hunchback monk who dabbles in heretical dialogue – and his master. The two men are tortured and finally confess to heresy and seem resigned to their fate, tied to a stake and torched as ordered by the manic witch-hunter.

Meanwhile, Brother William is closer to revealing the truth. As human infernos seem imminent, he and his novice finally gain access to the forbidden library and, within its labyrinthine passages, they hunt the poisoned pages of the book that will save the innocent and prove their theories correct.

In an online summation of the film, critic Nik Allen gave the film a general thumbs up and took great pains to explain why: '[*The Name of the Rose*] is told with sporadic narration and in flashback by Slater's novice and maintains an atmosphere lacking in many films of its time. The outlandish features of an ensemble cast are perfect for the subject matter and plot, Connery giving us one of his most assured performances and surely one of his favourites. Both Lonsdale and Abraham are excellent, along with Salvatore, the doomed hunchback played by Ron Perlman, who again is immense with his gargoyle-like features, comic yet mesmerising with his monkish appearance.

'The picture is strongest in its ability to portray strong images while maintaining a certain tenderness. The sometimes languid pace with hollow, eerie location are matched perfectly with poignant moments etched with comic undertones. The manner of Brother William can be found in Conan Doyle's iconic detective "Holmes", and with Slater as his "Watson" he is driven to solving the mystery with his Sherlockian instincts coming to the fore when mouthing the famous word "elementary".

'Religious themes are portrayed with a sense of hypocrisy, and indeed the very nucleus of holy belief is questioned continuously; the love of God can, it seems, be at least on a similar level to other forms of joy, as [demonstrated] when Connery states, "How peaceful life would be without love. How safe, how tranquil and how very dull."

'Slater's ultimate "sin", both natural and sexual, towards a female is given almost a green light by the wisdom of Connery, and in turn the hasty intercourse scene midway through is excellent and not out of place. The natural sensation of feeling emanating from Slater is a welcome angle on warmth and comfort within the human soul that can overcome darkness, tragedy and the religious code of infinite sorrow.'

Meanwhile, an article in Britain's *Empire* magazine summed up the general critical opinion that Christian, as a sixteen-year-old, 'showed admirable unself-consciousness as the shaven-headed Adson von Melk'.

But there was a sting in the tail. 'Nobody was providing any rules or discipline,' Christian says of that time. 'It was all really up in the air, and that first taste of freedom felt so good. I think I just did too much of it.'

Whether he did or didn't, it wasn't long before word got back to Mary Jo, who heard tales of parties, riotous fun and love affairs. 'Christian had chances to experiment, and I was unaware that he was,' she would ruefully remark years later.

All the same, and with such high praise for only his second big-screen outing, it should come as no surprise that Christian would next accept a role in Francis Ford Coppola's *Tucker: The Man and his Dream*. Once again, he became immediately starstruck with the company he would be keeping, rubbing shoulders with such heavy-hitters as Jeff Bridges, Joan Allen and Martin Landau. And to be in a film directed by such a great director as Coppola was simply the icing on the cake.

It was just two years before Coppola announced his intention to make another *Godfather* movie, and the word around Hollywood was that he was all but washed up – either that or he was deliberately squandering what was once considered one of the greatest talents in the business. A run of movies through the '80s, including *Tucker*, *The Outsiders*, *Rumblefish* and *Peggy Sue Got Married*, had all done pretty well at the box office, but, when distributors Orion Pictures announced that they expected to lose up to three million dollars on Coppola's 1984 *The Cotton Club*, it scarcely seemed worth pointing out that, at the time that they made the prediction, the film was still the second highest-grossing movie in America. The consensus was that Coppola sold movies on the strength of his name, but when people actually got to see his films they quickly backed away. It appeared to be desperation as much as anything else that finally convinced the director to shatter a resolution he had been keeping steadfastly for the last fifteen years not to out-sequel *The Godfather*.

Tucker, however, was a different story entirely. Most critics called it 'Francis Coppola: The Man and His Dream', observing that 'the flamboyant director has found more than a few parallels between himself and the visionary and ill-fated auto builder'. As Roger Ebert noted in his review, the real star of the movie was the car, and this isn't too surprising when one considers Coppola's fascination with the real-life Preston Tucker and his car, one of the biggest stories of 1948. Tucker was a dreamer and a rebel whose genius threatened a handful of the most powerful industrial giants in America and the politicians who protected them, and Coppola had dreamed of making a biopic about the man for at least ten years.

As many reviewers noted, however, the film doesn't quite come off. 'The worst scene in the movie is the most crucial,' observes Ebert, 'the scene where Tucker is scheduled to unveil his new beauty to the assembled American automobile press. We get a passage that's too long and too confused, a comedy of errors as the workmen try to push the big car up a ramp as a fire starts backstage and Tucker stands in front of the curtain, bamboozling the press. A little of this would have made the point; Coppola pushes it to distraction.'

Perhaps best described as a man before his time, Tucker

was a maverick innovator who dreamed of changing the world by introducing improved safety features and aerodynamic design to automobiles – or, as Roger Ebert summed it up, 'the man who actually succeeded in building fifty of them, just as he said he would, before he was shot down by the Big Three auto manufacturers from Detroit and their hired guns in Washington'.

But, questioned Ebert, 'would automotive history have been different if Tucker had put his dream into mass production? Probably not. The Tucker car would probably have thrived for a few late 1940 years and then joined the long, slow parade of the Hudson, the Kaiser, the Nash, the Studebaker, the Packard and all the other makes that your dad always warned you couldn't get parts for.'

For those unfamiliar with his story, Tucker was the dynamic inventor and charismatic salesman who pitched his idea for seatbelts, fuel injection and disc brakes to the purchasing public, and who, with the help of Abe Karatz, gathered enough funds to build a prototype of his futuristic car. He even began to pre-sell stock to dealerships across the country. Securing the world's largest manufacturing plant, he geared up for mass production of the auto, but, while post-war Americans were flush with enthusiasm for the Tucker Torpedo, with its 'low-slung, bullet-nose that looked like a discreet cross-breeding of the post-war Studebaker and the Batmobile', according to Ebert, outside sources began to put the squeeze on the little man with the big ideas. Unable to procure clay and steel for manufacturing, Tucker resorted to scrounging the city dump for needed materials while his handful of faithful designers and engineers worked around the clock to bring their prototype from paper to reality in a mere sixty days.

However, bigger trouble loomed ahead when the United States Securities and Exchange Commission began an investigation of Tucker's Corporation. When Michigan's Senator Homer Ferguson turned a cold shoulder on Tucker's request for help, the visionary creator relied on the support of his family and the legal efforts of a Mr Kirby to fight the highly publicised allegations of consumer fraud while holding together the struggling company.

As Coppola explains, 'Tucker's story reflects the hopes and dreams of America during the '40s after the Second World War, when the sky was the limit and we all thought we were going to live in a world of abundance with technological innovation. What happens in this movie probably goes on every month of the year. Tucker brought together a group of very talented individuals who fought for the right for his company to survive.'

Jeff Bridges, who played Tucker as an unpredictable, brilliant and passionate hero, agrees. 'He would call himself not an engineer but an imagineer. One of the things that you can see, watching the Tucker home movies, is how close he was to his family and how he included them in all aspects of his life.'

Certainly, added Joan Allen, who played Tucker's wife, 'Vera Tucker is very supportive of her husband. According to everything I've read and heard about the real family, Preston and Vera were able to sustain their romance throughout their marriage. While they're not perfect people, their love never diminished as the demands of their family and career increased.'

What Coppola perhaps liked most about the script and the story was how Tucker seemed to inspire those around him. As Martin Landau, who played the role of Tucker's associate and friend Abe Karatz, observed, 'Abe is a lonely person who shrouded himself in business most of his life, but, after meeting Tucker and his family, there's quite a metamorphosis.'

Equally inspirational to a point was the two-week period before shooting commenced, during which Coppola assembled the cast and crew on a sound stage for a ten-day schedule of read-throughs, rehearsals and watching original footage and home movies. And, as was his usual practice, Coppola shot the rehearsals on video for the purposes of improving on the performances. In his mind, by rehearsing the actors as if for a stage play, he could develop a sense of ensemble, which is one of his favourite methods of working, embracing everyone as if they were family.

Whether Christian enjoyed the experience of working in this way is questionable, as some years later he would tell *Premiere* magazine that he felt intimidated by the director's technique on set. 'I don't like to feel uncomfortable when I work, and I think that, if a director is somewhat legendary, he should be a little bit more understanding.' Although no one would be privy to exactly what he meant by this, and perhaps sensing that he shouldn't be saying anything at all, he still insists that 'Coppola was very, very sweet. A very sweet guy. I just had a little trouble.' And, once again, Christian's name is mentioned only in passing in the production notes for the film.

However, through his work on *Tucker: The Man and his Dream*, Christian did land himself a new publicist, Susan

Culley, who he met during filming and on whose counsel – probably more than that of anyone else in his life at that time – he would increasingly come to rely. 'We started working together at a time in my life when I needed to be mothered,' vowed Christian. That's not to say he had any less affection for his mother, however; time and again he would compare Mary Jo's role in his career to that of Rose Hovick, the mother of Natalie Wood's character in 1962's *Gypsy*. 'My nickname for her is Mama Rose,' he confides. 'She cares a great deal about what happens to me, and I care about her. Things are going smoothly right now. But *Gypsy* is one of her favourite films, so that's what I've had to contend with. There was a period of time where my mother was really involved in my career and my life. As good as it was, I just needed some independence. I couldn't have my mother running my life.'

As if to prove his point, by the time Christian was seventeen he had already moved out of his mother's house and in with his girlfriend, Kim Walker. The only problem was that they ran out of money, although he couldn't say how. 'All the money I made when I was growing up, I have no idea what I did with it or where I spent it. It's just all gone.'

Like Elvis before him, when things got desperate, the answer was simple: do a movie or two to get some money rolling in. And, although Christian's next project, *Gleaming the Cube*, would never win any Academy Awards, it did put him on the path to landing the film role that would transform his career forever.

As Christian said at the time of the film's release, in April 1988, 'I try to achieve something completely different with every film I do. *Gleaming the Cube* is a modern movie, so I tried to look really cool, but it remains to be seen if I pulled it off. I dyed my hair and let it grow long, pierced my ear and practised skateboarding for three months. It takes forever just to be able to stand on the thing. I skate well enough now to move around and make it look elegant for the movie, but three stunt guys did all my tricks for me.'

Gleaming the Cube tells the story of Brian Kelly (Christian), a standard-issue outcast teen rebel somewhat envious of the success of his adopted Vietnamese brother, Vinh, as both A-student and white sheep of the family. When Vinh apparently commits suicide, Brian refuses to believe it and sets out, on his skateboard, to find out what really happened and eventually to avenge his brother's murder. In his quest, Brian is aided by a cynical detective (Steven Bauer), assorted skating buddies and a beautiful Vietnamese girl.

On watching *Gleaming the Cube*, however, the *Washington Post*'s Richard Harrington was less than transformed by the experience. 'The plot, once uncovered, seems rather odd and convoluted, but maybe that's what director Graeme Clifford needed to justify the various skateboard chases. And while Clifford probably thinks *Gleaming the Cube* is about familial confusions, or Vietnamese refugee culture, it's really about chases and the ever-lengthening gaps in Hollywood between fantasy and reality. Slater is up to the role of Brian, vacuously rebellious until his brother's death leads him to clean up his act so he can infiltrate the bad guys' defences. To young teens, particularly fellow skateboarders, his efforts, both on the board and with a comb, will seem Herculean; the rest of the world will simply wonder what the film's title means.'

On that last subject, Clifford explained that the phrase featured in the movie's title is 'that special state where someone is operating at the peak of their own power. If Segovia is playing guitar perfectly, he's gleaming the cube. It's doing your absolute best or impossible best.'

Certainly, most journalists visiting the set were quick to note that, if nothing else, Christian was 'a pupil of the Jimmy Stewart Gee-Whiz School of Etiquette'. From his unassuming manner between takes, few would have argued with that summation, or would even guess that he appeared in virtually every frame of the movie, being present in more scenes than any of his co-stars.

Although *Gleaming the Cube* was neither a memorable movie nor a great one, and the critical response to it was lukewarm at best, director Graeme Clifford saw no cause to regret his decision in casting Christian. 'I'd seen most of what Christian had done and he's very self-assured. You can only accumulate so much experience in eighteen years, but he has a good grasp on reality and is uncommonly versatile.'

Chapter 4

Lethal Attraction

Three weeks before *Heathers* is due to open on 31 March 1989, Christian and Winona Ryder are about to appear at a promotional screening at a New York adult-school film class. The mostly suburban middle-aged audience is clearly troubled by the movie and its light-hearted treatment of diabolical themes, and many walk out halfway through, muttering their disapproval, shock and disdain.

Backstage, Christian and Winona are worried. She has an idea and whispers it to Christian. When the screening ends, they come out from behind the curtain and sit in chairs on stage, holding hands, and announce that they just got married the previous week in Las Vegas. Some class members applaud while others look befuddled, but Christian and Winona never drop the act or the conceit. Calling each other 'honey', their charm overpowers the critics.

A few days later, Winona is striding briskly through

Central Park wearing Christian's leather biker jacket. The zipper won't fasten, so her hands clasp it shut against the chilly spring breeze. She laughingly recalls the idea of marrying Christian. 'We talked about how we were going to do all the Hollywood marriage things,' she later remembers, 'like stage fights in restaurants, be really reclusive but then leak out everything. He'd cover my face when photographers came near, like Sean and Madonna.'

But, when Christian later went on a talk show and proposed to her on the air, Winona suddenly tired of the joke. 'People have been calling me about it,' she recalled. 'It doesn't sound too good. Marriage would be fun, but I don't think I'm ready for it yet.'

For Christian, though, it was no joke: he actually *did* fall in love with Winona. He and the actress playing the lead Heather, Kim Walker, had been dating since stage school. 'She was a terrific actress,' says Christian (Walker died in March 2001 from a brain tumour at the age of thirty-two), and Winona asserts that she and Christian 'never fooled around or anything during the movie'. But isn't it possible that they could have, given that it was during the thirty-two-day shoot that they fell for each other? It was the first time, after all, that Winona had become romantically involved with a leading man, but it probably wasn't the only time. Still doing the gossip rounds to this day are her oft-speculated flings with later co-stars Gary Oldman and Daniel Day-Lewis on and off the sets of *Bram Stoker's Dracula* and *The Age of Innocence*, respectively. If there is any truth to these rumours, perhaps it wouldn't be surprising if she and Christian did in fact have an affair during and after the film. According to Winona, however, their relationship didn't begin until after filming was completed and Christian had broken up with Kim. Even if they had 'fooled around' during filming, Christian would have found it easy to explain away, marvelling at 'the great chemistry you get going on a film set. You get to say all these things to a girl you never could normally.' Perhaps it was during the strip-croquet scene that the crush began. When both are lying naked, after 'boning away' on the croquet set, only covered by the clothing they had supposedly flung off during the match, to many this scene is evidence enough that the chemistry was already present.

As to whether or not they were actually dating, Winona continues, it was 'only for a couple of weeks, but it was too weird. When you're really good friends with somebody, it's hard when you try to make [it] work. It's bogus. It should just happen naturally. But he broke my heart, or I thought he did at the time.'

Christian, on the other hand, hoped that that wasn't true. 'She is a wild woman to work with,' he still affectionately admits today. 'She has a naivety, a vulnerability almost, that makes her attractive to be with and to watch.' She was, after all, the very reason why he wanted to do *Heathers* in the first place. 'I loved her since *Lucas*. She was so cute, so beautiful and so natural. She was very helpful and very professional. I could tell that she and I had some kind of chemistry.'

Winona agrees, 'We really have great on- and off-screen chemistry. He's one of the most brilliant actors I've ever worked with.' She can even remember the day he came in and read for the part of JD, his character in *Heathers*. 'A lot of guys came in and read the scene where I'm fake hanging, and they would do the whole monologue to me. I was just standing on this chair for two weeks and pretending I'm hanging while the actors do the speech. Some of them just didn't get the comedy of it, were really being very dramatic about it, and then Christian came in and he was perfect.'

But when one journalist asked Christian about a *People* magazine interview that quoted Winona as saying that he 'so scared' her that she once locked herself in her trailer, Christian admitted that, when not particularly sober, 'I was actually scary. Not the most positive guy in the world. A monster in some ways. Maybe I was born with anger. Maybe it was the weird, scary roles I was playing. I was dealing with a lot of shit, desperately trying to find out who the real me was. When I finally stopped trying to fight [to be somebody] I wasn't, I just sat back and said, "This is the guy I'm stuck with. I've got to be happy with it, or why go on?"'

Part of 'that shit', as Christian puts it, started in the same year that *Heathers* was released. Between Christmas and New Year, on 29 December 1989 – coincidentally just hours after Winona collapsed in Rome and was forced to drop out of *The Godfather Part III* – Los Angeles police observed a Saab 900 being driven erratically in west Hollywood. The driver was Christian, on his way home from a nightclub and doing 50mph in a 35mph zone. The cops pulled the car over and what happened next established a pattern of anarchic behaviour that would periodically affect the next seven years of Christian's life. Instead of simply pulling over, he began a ludicrously short-lived car chase that ended mere seconds after it had begun in a back alley, of all places, with Christian crashing into two telephone poles, abandoning his vehicle, attempting to flee over a fence and, in the scuffle – deliberately or otherwise – kicking one of the officers in the face. 'I thought I was Batman,' he said at the time. 'I had the same mentality, but not,' he joked, 'the utility belt.'

Christian was charged with evading the police, driving under the influence of alcohol, driving with a suspended licence and assault with a deadly weapon – specifically, his cowboy boots. And, with another drink-driving conviction from the previous year already on the books, Christian was sentenced to serve ten days in prison, which he served just over six months later in July 1990. This brief sojourn behind bars was followed by a ninety-day stint in a voluntary rehabilitation programme, from which he discharged himself on day seven. For the first few months of the following year, he also attended regular meetings of Alcoholics Anonymous. 'It's hard enough to be a parent, much less the parent of a movie star,' laments Mary Jo. 'When you love someone so much and you see that they're falling and you're trying to stop it, you know they have to fall because it's part of life experience.'

Part of that life experience included some court-ordered community service, for which Christian decided to try working behind the scenes, directing *The Laughter Epidemic*, a children's musical that ran at the Westwood Playhouse in Los Angeles, raising $200,000 in the process for the charity the Pediatric AIDS Foundation. 'People tend to ignore that,' he complained. 'They like to focus on the darker stuff. It's more interesting, I guess.'

Dan Lauria, Christian's childhood father figure and friend, agreed. It was a period that was a particularly tough one for everyone in Christian's life. 'The reason Christian and I get along is because, during that time, I said, "I'm here when you call,"' he remembers. 'I didn't bug him, so I always got the calls after the fact. When he went to AA meetings, that's when I had to go, just to get him started, until he got his sponsor.'

Although the roots of much of his wild behaviour lay in the time he spent on film sets as a boy, Christian was still indulging in what he called his 'old-time late nights'. On one occasion, he remembers, 'It was about three in the morning and I was with this great girl. We were drinking and having a wonderful time when she mentioned to me that she had Jack Nicholson's telephone number. So I was like, "Great, great. I'll give him a call." Well, I got him on the phone and said, "Jack, this is Christian Slater. I just finished shooting *Heathers*. It hasn't come out yet, but I do this tribute to you in it." I heard a click from his end of the telephone line, but I wanted to impress the girl, so I went into a five-minute spiel: "Yeah, we'll play tennis sometime," and all that. I finished and paused for a second, and this voice suddenly went, "Eh hah." He was listening to me the whole time! I don't know if he thought I was completely insane or trying to impress somebody or what, but I couldn't take it, so I just hung up on him. I hung up on Jack Nicholson. It was a moment of clarity, like, "What have I done? I've just ruined my career."'

But the soul-searching often gave way to exuberance. 'I'm very mischievous,' he says proudly. 'A couple of days ago, I ran around and stole the doormats from my neighbours. I just wanted to stir things up a little. I still have them.'

According to *People Weekly*, one of his favourite pastimes

was Nintendo, and the Westwood apartment he now shares with an 85lb Akita named Winston could pass for a branch of US toy store FAO Schwarz. 'I spend a lot of time in toy stores,' he admits. Indeed, his mother recalls that, after shooting the explicit love scene in *The Name of the Rose*, Christian 'went home and played with his *Star Wars* figures'. For Christian, being a ladies' man with a boy's psyche is just fine. 'Maybe if I have time for myself, I can do stuff like take cooking classes and grow as a person and all that malarkey, but for now I just don't want to grow up.'

Perhaps Winona didn't, either. Back in Central Park, she took a seat on a park bench and stared out at the boating lake where, years later, she would film the opening scenes for *Autumn in New York* with Richard Gere. But, for now, and just a few months away from meeting her first true love, Johnny Depp, she suddenly looked tired. She had been doing *Heathers* promotions for a few weeks now. Waking up at dawn to do the *Today* show, for instance, seemed to indicate that, while her fame had finally caught up with her, it was beginning to take its toll.

In the two years prior to filming *Heathers*, Winona had already made a significant mark on the big screen, from her debut as the love-sick teenager in *Lucas* to a girl who enters a tender but doomed relationship with a mentally disabled boy (played by Rob Lowe) in *Square Dance*, playing supernatural comedy in Tim Burton's *Beetlejuice* and starring opposite Robert Downey Jr and Kiefer Sutherland in *1969*. Born in Minnesota and raised in northern California, one of her many goals at the time of filming *Heathers* was to study literature and history at Trinity College, Ireland, and to devote more of her off-screen time to screenwriting and film-making.

In fact, it was just before filming *1969* that Winona received the *Heathers* script (from a friend 'who wasn't supposed to give it out') and, after reading it, announced that she intended to follow *1969* with the role of Veronica Sawyer in the movie. The only trouble was that her agency at the time, Triad Artists, had never heard of it. The agency then tried hard to dissuade her from making the picture, just as Christian's agent did with him.

From the beginning, *Heathers* was considered to be a bizarre script that no one was ever going to make, see or release, but it was too late; Winona was adamant that it would be her next movie. Christian, too, was determined to make the film: 'I was just starting out so I thought it was an interesting, different, dark movie. But, when I told my mother about it, she was, like, "No. Don't go near it."'

So exactly what was considered so bad about *Heathers*? Was it the fact that screenwriter Daniel Waters and director Michael Lehmann's film was intending to twist the subject of teen suicide, at that time a public concern, becoming one of the leading causes of juvenile fatalities? In 1989, fully seven years before the self-destruction of Nirvana vocalist Kurt Cobain put an entire nation's worth of parents on suicide alert, teen suicide was hitting the headlines more and more regularly, most prominently in a couple of cases where rock 'n' roll music seemed to be implicated, with songs with titles like 'Shoot to Thrill' and 'Suicide Solution' being pursued into the courts.

Although Daniel Waters later admitted that his script was

'making fun out of teen suicide', it was far from making a joke out of it. What it was really doing, Winona explained, was criticising 'the way in which society has made teen suicide seem romantic'. Indeed, it was a subject that, for Winona, struck close to home: one of her own high-school classmates in Petaluma had committed suicide. Winona went to great pains to explain that what happens in *Heathers* is precisely what happened in real life, a viewpoint she still holds today. 'People made fun of her. People were horrible to her. She was called everything from a freak, a witch, just a girl who dressed differently who was kind of goth.' Then, after she killed herself, 'Everybody's her best friend. Everybody talks about how wonderful and beautiful and great and artistic she was. Her funeral was huge and they gave her a spread in the yearbook, just like in *Heathers*.'

Perhaps that last fact alone should have warned both Christian and Winona away from the film. 'It's not a funny subject,' they were told, 'and people won't find it funny. They'll think it's distasteful.' Interestingly enough, neither Winona nor Christian thought it was.

'I remember wanting to kill some girls in high school, but would never have dreamed of doing it,' Winona recalls. 'But it's such a difficult time in a person's life, and I think almost everyone has fantasies like that. Although the film is an exaggeration, the cliques and all the pranks in the film were like those I experienced in school. I think it's the insecurity of students that prompts them to be cruel to others. The results can be humiliating and devastating if you're not a member of one of the cliques, which I detested with a passion,'

For Christian, the prospect of playing the bad guy

appealed to him most. In contrast to his earlier roles, the character of JD was a gift. 'He wants to make a statement, be a cult leader,' Christian observes. 'He is every kid's fantasy gone one step too far, every kid who is not popular and has dreams of knocking off those who bug him, and then getting away with it. Wouldn't that be a dream come true? But he is confused and motivated by the excitement he has created at school and goes off at the deep end. I just made him as crazy and weird as I possibly could.'

Six years after the film's release, Christian's performance in *Heathers* was still drawing rave reviews from journalists, among them Steven Daly, who in the January 1995 issue of *The Face* noted, 'Critics were dazzled by Slater's gimlet-eyed performance; they spoke in hushed tones of the boy's dazzling confidence, his once-in-a-decade potential and his imminent A-list status. He was nineteen, pin-up cute and possessed of a magnetism that marked him out as the Boy Most Likely. And it didn't hurt that he was acting opposite Winona Ryder, that year's Girl Most Likely.'

Spin magazine's Jonathan Bernstein agreed: 'As Jason Dean, straddling and eventually teetering over the line that separates smouldering dreamboat rebel from drooling psycho, he gave the movie its meat. His cheerful offing of the offending elite, and subsequent stagings of the slayings as suicidal reactions to adolescent angst, reeked of an audacity that had critics calling *Heathers* the *Dr. Strangelove* of teen movies.'

Even though director Lehmann acknowledges that his leading man had 'more than a trace of Nicholson', Slater admits that a lot of the zany devilry he exhibited was inspired by a different actor entirely. 'My father really had a great deal of influence on how that character was played. There were certain characteristics of his that I picked up, and a lot of those, I guess, resemble the stuff that Jack does. Because my relationship with my father was so confusing, when I saw Jack Nicholson in a movie, I just felt a connection there.'

Distasteful or not, *Heathers* wastes no time in introducing its main characters: three girls, all named Heather, who like nothing better than a nice game of croquet, and Veronica, who they have buried up to her neck in the garden and whose head they are using as a hoop. At that moment *Heathers* looks like nothing more than a twisted take on 1,000 other high-school movies, but imperceptibly it begins to take on darker tones.

It is quickly established that the Heathers – played by Kim Walker, Lisanne Falk and Shannen Doherty – are the clique at Westerburgh High, renowned for their sadistic pecking order of bestowing favour or insult on whomever they chose. Winona, as Veronica, is the only partially willing courtier they pull along in their wake. She is also an expert in crafting other people's handwriting, a skill whose usefulness soon becomes apparent to the Heathers.

When the vilest of the Heathers (Walker) decides that the school fatty, Martha Dumptruck, needs a pick-me-up, she instructs Veronica to write a pornographic love letter in the hand of her polar opposite, the school jock, Kurt Kelly. But the boot will soon be on the other foot, of course, when Veronica and her newly acquired boyfriend, the distinctly sinister JD (Christian), poison that same vile Heather with a kitchen-cleaner cocktail as a hangover cure. It takes mere seconds for Veronica to craft the suicide note.

For Veronica, Heather's death is the culmination of several months of increasingly bilious journal-keeping. For JD, however, it is something else entirely. The character of JD, the son of a demolition worker whose wife killed herself in one of his controlled explosions, is rooted somewhere between Satan and Jack Nicholson, a demon lover who is simply fulfilling Veronica's secret fantasies. And, with her own journal entries to back him up, there is little evidence that she can offer to the contrary.

The couple's next victims are the school jocks who have been spreading a particularly sordid fiction about Veronica's sexual partiality of having two guys in her mouth at once. Luring them to a patch of woodland at dawn, JD and Veronica shoot them by using what JD tells Veronica are special tranquiliser bullets that 'break the surface of the skin enough to cause a little blood but no real damage', but of course he's lying. Once again, he is simply executing his devilish plot, this time to stage a 'repressed homosexual suicide pact', surrounding the bodies with artefacts suggesting much the same, including, of course, another of Veronica's crafted suicide notes, this one announcing 'a forbidden love to an uncaring and un-understanding world'.

But are things really going according to plan? Veronica suddenly realises that, in death, their victims' popularity has only grown. In fact, the deaths have captured the entire town's attention. Local-TV crews visits the school to report on a mourning ceremony dreamed up by a hippie teacher, and the biggest hit on local radio is a song titled 'Teen Suicide – Don't Do It' by a band called Big Fun.

The bulk of the film's impact is delivered in the first half of the movie. Abruptly shifting its emphasis halfway through, the remainder of the film is devoted to JD and Veronica's personal but very different realisations that suicide itself is not the problem. The dead Heather, after all, was simply succeeded by a live one, and one jock is much the same as another. That, they agree, is the nature of society. But is it an unchangeable fact? Veronica thinks it is; JD merely reckons that they haven't tried hard enough and by now is hatching his most brilliant plan yet, a 'Woodstock for the '80s', circulating a series of spurious petitions around the school, collecting signatures for a mass suicide note that will be 'the kind of thing to affect a generation'.

The climax of the movie is devoted to Veronica's battle to stop JD from executing his devilish plot, which in turn leads to the film's only genuine act of self-immolation, when he blows himself up with the bomb with which he intended to take out the school.

According to Waters, the film originally had a far better finale, ending with the school prom in heaven, where the punch being served is the blue drain cleaner that Heather Chandler drank and the musical entertainment is provided by Martha Dumptruck. Although there were plans to shoot this ending, the powers-that-be at New World Pictures considered it too dark for the teen marketplace and demanded it be substituted for a new, upbeat ending.

By the time the film finally made it onto the screens for its opening weekend, it was already producing a mixed critical reaction. *The Nation*'s critic noted that '*Heathers*, a new comedy, lets you fulfil one of the core fantasies of adolescence: seeing all the popular kids in their graves.' The *Chicago Sun Times*'s Roger Ebert, meanwhile, observed that 'the movie is shot in bright colours and set in a featherweight high-school environment in which dumb sight gags are allowed to coexist with the heavy stuff', although he wasn't sure whether the film was 'a black comedy or a cynical morality play', concluding his review by pointing out that 'teenagers will understand it best'.

At the other end of the spectrum, however, were those critics who missed the movie's point altogether. One bluntly described *Heathers* as 'a would-be absurdist farce intended as a send-up of all those high-school films about basically adorable teenagers, with which we associate John Hughes, Molly Ringwald and a bunch of other names I would gladly never have heard of.' But perhaps what this reviewer missed was the fact that 1989 was the year the stock market had crashed and the glib spend-spend-spend mentality of the '80s was over. While Ringwald had become a star by always longing to be cool in movies like *Sixteen Candles* and *Pretty In Pink* (two of Christian's favourites, incidentally), Slater and Ryder personified the theory that cookie-cutter cool now sucked big-time. And, in the process, they became stars.

Another reviewer not to get the picture was *The Times*'s Shelia Benson, who complained, 'No amount of production sheen or acting skill seems excuse enough for the film's scabrous morality or its unprincipled viciousness.'

Mired between such contradictory viewpoints, *Heathers* was by no means a box-office smash, its gross of a little over

$1 million ranking it a meagre 165th on the year's most successful movies listing. On the midnight circuit, however it could do no wrong. In America, in particular, the film acquired such a cult following that some showings reported audience members shouting out dialogue from the movie while the on-screen action unfolded. Moans of 'Fuck me gently with a chainsaw' and 'I love my dead gay son!' became familiar quotes across the country. If it's true that every generation gets the cult it deserves, there could be no better successor to *A Clockwork Orange* than *Heathers*.

Two years after the film's release, it was even turned into a stage play by students from the same high school that Winona had attended in Petaluma. Sharing the same critical objection that the film had received in some quarters, the only real downside for the self-named Inappropriate Players was the fact that high-school principal Frank Lynch didn't want it staged on the school campus because of the language and content in the script, so he banned it, branding the play as being 'inappropriate for high-school students', even though some lines had been cut from the pre-shooting script that teen director Todd (now Tawd b) Dorenfeld had obtained from Script City in Hollywood.

Dorenfeld was the brains behind the production. Not only did he turn the script into a stage version, later having to excuse himself from class to run home in order to take a call from Daniel Waters to explain why 'some punk kid was trying to do his film on a school stage', but he also took on the role that Christian had played in the film. 'I studied his work like one would study a snail crossing the street,' he recalls today. 'I looked closely at why he made those

Nicholson choices. I took a kind of pop-history approach. Jack was the human that played the hero in *Cuckoo's Nest* on the screen, and that role to me was what Slater's character was trying to portray. The character, after all, had no personality of his own; he couldn't separate his politics from his emotions. He needed to pretend who he wanted to be. So, doing the Nicholson/James Dean/hydro-baby teenager was perfect; it made him cool. So I did that. I did Slater.'

Despite Dorenfeld's praise, it is perhaps amusing to consider that there was a time when Michael Lehmann wasn't too sure about Christian's ability to pull off the character of JD. 'You look at him and think, This guy shouldn't be a movie star; he's got these rounded cheekbones and this funny little grin on his face and those eyebrows that go up and those eyes that squint,' he recalls. 'I remember turning to our casting directors, who were women, and saying, "What do you think? Are girls going to like him?" And everybody nodded their heads and said, "You bet!"'

By the time the students were on the verge of surrendering their ambitions of staging the play as the spring school production, the school's drama teacher, Robert Liroff, who had believed in Dorenfeld's enthusiasm, choice, pitch and rewriting from the start, continued to do his best to schmooze the school's governors to withdraw the ban. He got nowhere until Raymond Jax, a professional producer of concerts, plays and events whose daughter Taliesyn was playing one of the Heathers in the floundering production, came flying to the rescue to produce the play off campus, with Liroff's full support, and that of Tom Gaffey at the Phoenix Theater in downtown Petaluma. Then, as now,

Gaffey managed the Phoenix as a popular hangout for teens who either had nowhere else to go, didn't want to go home to abusive or absent parents, or just wanted a comfortable place in which to spend time away from the watchful eyes of local police. With permission from Hollywood's TransAtlantic Entertainment granted to perform the play based on the screenplay of the film, and with a telegram of encouragement and support from Winona, Michael Lehmann and Daniel Waters (also including Winona's regret that her schedule would not allow her to break free to attend), the play eventually ran for three nights in June 1991.

Ten months earlier, Christian's latest film, *Pump Up the Volume*, had just been released. It was another of those projects that he'd made against the advice of his agent and other Hollywood insiders – and just as well he did. No sooner was it playing across the country than it began gaining as much momentum as *Heathers* had, only in this film Christian's teen rebellion was far less fatal.

Although Christian was pleased with the recognition that *Heathers* brought him, he was hoping that *Pump Up the Volume* would distance him from the gleefully evil student he had previously portrayed. To many, the film was only one notch down from *Heathers*, while to others it was one notch up. *Empire* magazine, however, considered that 'both were basically the same film', with Westerburgh High now Hubert Humphrey High and Winona Ryder now Samantha Mathis. Even so, the general consensus was that, like *Heathers*, *Pump Up the Volume* was a smart, perceptive and thought-provoking look at issues that perhaps the average teen or high-school film failed to address. The characters were far more like real people one would expect to find walking through school halls and nothing like the cardboard cut-outs with which Hollywood typically populates classrooms.

It's almost ironic that the movie had been doing the Hollywood rounds for years before finding a home owing to the fact that its director and writer, Allan Moyle, couldn't think of anyone suitable to play the lead role of Mark Hunter, aka Happy Harry Hard-on. Despite Lehmann's initial concerns over Christian playing JD in *Heathers*, Moyle had no such worries about casting him. As far as he was concerned, the day he met Christian was the day he found someone who could carry off the dual demands of the role to do the character justice. 'I like to think of him as a combination of Lenny Bruce and Holden Caulfield, so, when we met Christian, I finally saw the character come alive,' Moyle remembers. 'Christian has an ineffable blend of innocence and power that makes him thrilling to watch.'

Like *Heathers*, *Pump Up the Volume* told a story of troubled youth, where Mark Hunter is an intelligent high-school student whose move from New York to Arizona has thrown him into a profound state of depression and isolation. In fact, Mark is such a shy, introverted kid that, now that he's left behind all his old friends, he can't seem to make any new ones. As he puts it in the movie, 'He could be that anonymous nerd sitting across from you in the chem lab, staring at you so hard. Then, when you turn around, he tries to smile, but the smile just comes out all wrong. You just think, How pathetic. Then he just looks away and never looks back at you again.'

Mark's father is a high-school commissioner who sold out

his '60 s dreams and ideals and relocated to typical American suburbia with his wife, Mark's mother. The pair have no idea who their son really is, or at least not well enough to understand the depth of his psychological wound. By day, Mark is a conscientious student whose writing teacher, Jan Emerson (Ellen Greene), praises his work, and who attracts the attention of his goth classmate, Nora Diniro (Samantha Mathis). But every night at ten, Mark, with a voice disguiser, transforms himself into Happy Harry Hard-on, a pirate-radio DJ who broadcasts via his shortwave set.

Attracting followers to his nightly radio show like a messiah, Happy Harry's programme can last anywhere from five minutes to five hours and features anti-mainstream music, profane rants against school and society, and faked masturbation sessions. He is both the echo and embodiment of teenage defiance, urging his listeners to battle the faculty at every turn, either to defend or regain freedom – especially when he reminds his fellow students 'to eat their cereal with a fork and do their homework in the dark'. His rantings are enough to appal most adults who hear it, but they serve as a magnet for teenagers. Soon Happy Harry is a local legend, but the moral conscience of the community begins to worry about his influence. 'They say I'm disturbed,' he tells his listeners in one broadcast. 'Well, of course I'm disturbed. I mean, we're all disturbed. And if we're not, why not? Doesn't this blend of blindness and blandness make you want to do something crazy? Then why not do something crazy? It makes a helluva lot more sense than blowing your brains out.'

Unfortunately, and against all the odds, this is exactly what one young listener does after engaging Harry in an on-air conversation about suicide and kills himself immediately afterwards. When the news breaks the following morning, community leaders, searching for someone to blame, elect to go after Happy Harry rather than the cold, emotionally distant parents of the dead boy. The rest of the movie is then devoted to the ensuing witch-hunt, bent on bringing Happy Harry down and off the air.

As in *Heathers*, in *Pump Up the Volume* Christian became romantically involved with his co-star. Despite the insistence of Hollywood gossip, the relationship apparently developed towards the end of filming, and not, as some believe, during the love scene, in which Samantha Mathis goes topless.

In fact, the decision to cast Samantha was equally as instinctive as casting Christian. Moyle had seen many young actresses before he met her. 'Our casting director, Judith Holstra, knew Samantha, and suggested we see her,' he recalls, 'and the minute she came in we knew she was Nora.'

Born in Brooklyn, New York, to actress Bibi Besch, by the time she was sixteen Samantha had landed a role in the short-lived American television series *Aaron's Way*. Then a feature-film debut in *Forbidden Sun* led to her being cast opposite Christian, which in turn garnered her the leading role in the country-western film *The Thing Called Love*. Although the film was a critical and box-office disappointment, it did bring Samantha true love when she began to date her co-star River Phoenix during filming. Unfortunately, her love wasn't enough to end his addiction to drugs and, on Halloween night, 1993, Phoenix overdosed and died on the sidewalk outside Johnny Depp's Viper Room with Samantha looking on, devastated.

But shooting *Pump Up the Volume*, Samantha remembers, 'was a magical time for me. It was my first feature film and I loved the character so much, and to get the opportunity to play her and work with Christian, who was someone I really admired and a peer of mine, was really wonderful. And Allan Moyle created a really unique environment while shooting that film. He's a real artist and was really interested in having a very collaborative film-making experience. This is a guy who started having parties at the production office six weeks before we were shooting so people would get to know each other. He wanted everyone to be inspired and inspiring. So it was a really wonderful, embracing experience, the environment he created.'

Watching the movie now, she admits that it's 'very prophetic of what happened in the next ten years. Christian's pirate-radio station was something the government could shut down, but they could never do the same to the internet, which was just on the horizon at that point.'

Moyle modelled artistic, avant-garde poet Nora on the acclaimed singer/songwriter Patti Smith, and after she landed the role Samantha read everything she could about Smith and listened to all her records. She also began to keep a journal for Nora, write poetry, buy art supplies and draw just as Nora would in the film. The most obvious thing she did, however, was dye her natural blonde hair a dark reddish brown. 'We all saw Nora as a brunette,' Moyle said at the time. 'The character is a renegade and a self-made artist. She definitely has a darker look.'

Samantha had a great deal of input into the rest of Nora's persona. 'I thought Nora would wear animal pins, so we got a lot of those,' she recalls, laughing at the memory. She also confesses that 'Allan also encouraged me to wear some of my own clothes', just as her friend Winona Ryder did for *Beetlejuice*. 'I even helped design Nora's room. It's a hodgepodge of different things: a big old dead tree that serves as a clothing rack, MC Escher prints on the walls.'

The chemistry between the fledging love affair of Mark and Nora is extremely important, and Moyle felt he was fortunate in finding exactly the right balance. 'Christian and Samantha first met at the screen test. They have a great rapport, and it really comes across on film. The magical thing is that you feel like they're in love. Luckily, he and Samantha were actually falling in love at that time. It was nerve-racking for me, because they could fall out of love just as quickly, but what could I say?'

Moyle also kept quiet about Christian visiting a number of college radio stations and spending time at his uncle's radio station on Cape Cod to learn as much as he could about radio before filming got under way, so that he could get a feel for the character he was playing. He also developed what he considered a Superman/Clark Kent persona. As he pointed out, 'During the day in school, Mark is a shy kid who wears glasses, but, when he takes them off at night, he turns into this wild rebel, this incredibly horny lunatic. In fact, just your basic, average kid, which of course I related to.'

Although Christian had very little high-school experience to draw upon because, as he puts it, 'I had tutors for the last three years of high school because I was working so much', he does admit that there are similarities between the character of Mark and himself. 'I'm very shy and reserved at times, and I tend to voice my opinions quietly in a room with one other person or by myself. Although I used to go into my trailer if I was pissed off about something and just started screaming to myself, it made no sense, but I thought it was sort of cute, in a way.'

One major difference between Mark and Christian, though, is their musical tastes. While Mark spins a steady barrage of cutting-edge tunes, Christian's tastes, surprisingly, tend towards the traditional. As he proudly points out, however, both kinds of music often carry the same life-sustaining message: 'Allan and I got together and tried to work some stuff out, but always threw out ideas like Frank Sinatra,' he recalls. 'I love that song "That's Life". It's become my theme song. If you ever get really pissed off, learn the words to that song: "I've been a puppet, a pauper, a pirate, a poet, a pawn and a king./I've been up and down and over and out and I know one thing./Each time I find myself flat on my face,/I pick myself up and get back in the race." Now that's a good, healthy, admirable way to go.'

After *Pump Up the Volume*, Mike Ovitz, the head of Creative Artists Management (the agency representing Christian at that time) told him that he'd better get a hobby or something, 'because you're going to have a lot of time sitting around and waiting for some great project to come'. Despite such reservations, however, and still relying on the counsel of publicist Susan Culley, Christian's next project came along a lot sooner than he or his agent had anticipated.

Chapter 5

Guns, Bows and Arrows

P*ump Up the Volume* wasn't the only movie featuring Christian that was on release in August 1990 (most people forgot about *The Wizard* and *Tales from the Darkside* before their seats were even cold). The sequel to the 1998 hit *Young Guns*, yet another revisionist version of the Billy the Kid legend, *Young Guns II* was considered necessary due to the success of its predecessor, due perhaps to the cast of the original, comprising young brat packers and Gen-X stars including, among others, Emilio Estevez and Kiefer Sutherland. And, although Christian could be added to that list, it's strange – especially after his breakthrough role in *Heathers* – that he is again barely mentioned in the production notes or in the reviews published on the film's release. Nor were there any references to Christian's commentary about his role in the film – that of Billy the Kid's pal, crazy Arkansas Dave Rudabaugh – nor even a press junket interview to tie in with the new film's release.

One year later, however, when *Interview* magazine caught up with Christian for a July 1991 feature, he did talk about riding horses in the film. 'I had never ridden as much as I did during the making of that movie. We rode every day, and what really got me into it was this bitch of a horse that I had no rehearsal time with. I mounted it and *voom!* Suddenly I rode off into the plains, hanging from the saddle, zooming past cactuses, and the camera crew loved it. They're going, "Wow, he's really moving. Good for Christian." Well, the next time I had to get on that horse, I was petrified, but I knew that I had to show him who was boss. I grabbed hold of the mane and the reins and, when he started doing his little dance, flaring his nostrils, I whacked him in the back of the neck. *Pow!* He didn't fuck with me for the rest of the movie. You know, I like to win. I'm not going to be beaten by a fucking horse or by anybody else who gets in my way.'

It's strange that, despite featuring such a powerful list of young Hollywood in the line-up, the film was received less than favourably by most critics. One of those critical of the movie was Roger Ebert, who noted (perhaps correctly) in his review that the movie had 'the feeling that the screenplay was put together out of various standard western elements without any clear idea of where the movie was headed, or why'. Certainly, continued Ebert, 'the final shootout when Garrett and his men surround the gang is a disappointment. An event immortalised in other films (such as *Gunfight At The OK Corral*, *The Left-Handed Gun* and *Pat Garrett and Billy The Kid*) is trivialised in this one.'

However, according to John Fusco, screenwriter of both

movies, both *Young Guns* and *Young Guns II* were probably the most accurate depiction of the boy bandit ever seen on film. The sequel, as far as Fusco was concerned, was 'the historical continuation of the Lincoln County War story and, specifically, the story of Billy the Kid and his gang. In *Young Guns*, we see Billy transform, in the public eye, from a juvenile delinquent to a folk hero. In *Young Guns II*, we see the legend growing under Billy's feet so fast and furious that he himself can't keep up with it.'

The story of *Young Guns II* centres on how the legend that The Kid has become puts him on a collision course with his old friend, Pat Garrett, outlaw-turned-lawman, who has been hired by cattle barons and politicians to hunt down his buddy and kill him. It is, in short, the standard cat-and-mouse tale of friendship and betrayal, set against the backdrop of the Old West.

In retrospect, the idea that Fusco would end up writing and executive-producing two films about Billy the Kid shouldn't have been surprising; it had been a twenty-year interest for him. 'I've had a fascination with the Wild West since I was ten years old – the life, the mining towns, the outlaws. I don't know why it was such a magnet, but it really drew me in, and one of the first characters I became fascinated with was Billy the Kid. When I saw that first tintype photo of Billy, the only confirmed photo that exists, I was surprised. I'd seen him played in films by Johnny Mack Brown, Audie Murphy, Paul Newman and Kris Kristofferson, and they played him as a black-clad ladies' man who whistled sad ballads, was left-handed and rode off into the sunset.' But, continues Fusco, 'he always kept that sense of humour. When he was sentenced to death by Judge Bristol, the judge said to him, "William H Bonney, you are sentenced to be hanged by the neck until you are dead, dead, dead!" And Billy turned to him, right in the courtroom, and said, "Well, sir, you can go to hell, hell, hell!" Even in the face of death, he was able to laugh. Another appealing trait of his was that he was extremely loyal. He was this incredible free spirit who loved the idea of himself, but he also loved his pals. He held his friends very dear.'

Fusco's fascination was eventually communicated to the rest of the cast, especially Emilio Estevez, who returned to reprise his role as Billy the Kid in *Young Guns II*. 'I immersed myself in this character six to eight weeks before we started shooting,' Estevez recalls. 'John Fusco and I even drove down to Lincoln, the town where Billy wreaked so much havoc. I really became fascinated with who this guy was, and how he lived, and how he dealt with the Old West his whole life. He had an incredible zest for life, and I really look at him as an original American rebel.'

Displaying much the same passion for the character as Christian, Estevez continues, 'I think we're fascinated by rebellious characters. We're still fascinated by James Dean, and you could say Billy was like a movie star, to some extent. He was a media celebrity. We were fascinated by media celebrity then as we are now. A measure of Billy's celebrity is that this is the forty-eighth film to be made about him, and I think we have gotten as close to whom Billy really was as possible.'

Above all, like most people, Estevez sees Billy the Kid's boundless ego as part of his charm and part of his downfall. 'He really knew no restraints. I think he was very taken by himself, with his own personality and his own celebrity, which is one of the reasons he never left New Mexico. He said that, if he went down to Old Mexico, he'd just be another gringo and no one would recognise him.

'What is intriguing about Billy is that he wasn't about to be caged in by barbed wire or by the cattle kings who were controlling the territory, or by the governor, or by anybody else trying to tell him what to do. He would just turn around and go the opposite way. He constantly defied authority. That's the way he lived his life. And, of course, that is how and why he died.'

In July 1991, less than a year after *Young Guns II* hit the cinema, Christian's next project, a role in *Robin Hood: Prince of Thieves*, was another movie not to be received well by the critics. Most thought it preposterous from the outset, but Roger Ebert was particularly chastening. Having admitted that he found many problems with the movie, especially with how Kevin Costner lacked everything that we normally associate with the character, he opined that it was 'a murky, unfocused, violent and depressing version of the classic story, with little of the light-heartedness and romance we expect from Robin Hood. [The fact that it was] shot mostly at night and in gloomy forests, beneath overcasts or by flickering firelight or in gloomy dungeons … makes the action scenes almost impossible to follow.'

Ebert apparently wasn't the only one who was unhappy about Costner's performance. Alan Rickman, who was cast as the mad, ranting, glam-rock Sheriff of Nottingham, was a huge popular hit with audiences and completely upstaged Costner.

Maybe one of the reasons why Costner's nose was put so far out of joint by Rickman was, according to one movie insider, that 'at first Costner didn't really know who Alan was. The name meant nothing to him. But, when they started filming, Costner went into a sulk because he suddenly realised what a formidable actor Alan was. Costner has this reputation for being incredibly well endowed, physically – it made his name in Hollywood –and that's why he wouldn't wear traditional tights in the role of Robin of Locksley; frankly, it would have been too obvious. So they made him a pair of breeches instead. The joke is that, even though Costner is supposed to have the biggest willy in Hollywood, Alan Rickman still upstaged him with that wonderful roguish quality. He just had such a powerful presence.'

Despite such dramas on set and the critical objections, however, the film still remains Christian's most successful movie yet. In a June 1991 edition of the *Washington Post*, critic Desson Howe offered a completely opposing and possibly more concise summary of the film than Ebert. 'The film looks like big money. It has stars, it's based on a classic and foolproof story and it's an exhilarating couple of hours. It fills the entertainment megabill utterly.'

The idea of making yet another retelling of the story of Robin Hood was the brainchild of screenwriters and producers John Watson and Pen Densham, who for five years held a constant passion to deliver the sort of script on English folklore that Hollywood would take to its heart. 'After talking about it for so long, we didn't really get writing together on it until the start of 1989,' Watson recalls. 'Pen suddenly hit on the idea of Robin being captured while on the crusades, that we should start with him in jail, escaping. During the escape, two things happen to shape the story: his best friend is killed, who turns out to be the brother of Maid Marian, and his dying wish is that Robin should look after his sister. He also escapes with another prisoner, a Moor, and saves his life. The Moor believes that he should stay with Robin until he has a chance to save his life too. We felt this was a fresh and exciting way of reintroducing the Robin Hood story.'

Morgan Creek Productions were among the first to be crucially involved in the ten-hour decision to acquire Watson and Densham's script. David Nicksay, then president of production at Morgan Creek, remembers, 'I heard through the grapevine that there was a very hot screenplay on Robin Hood, so I arranged to receive the script on 13 February 1990. I took it home that evening and asked two members of our staff to also take it home. We all read it overnight, discussed it the next morning and, by noon of 14 February – St Valentine's Day – we determined to get it. We all thought that this was commercial, distinctive and great fun, and that we could really make it work.'

Remaking *Robin Hood* was just as much a gamble as attempting to find a new angle for a film on the Billy the Kid legend. Based on one of England's best-loved heroes, a figure who had already spawned a barrage of popular movies and two television series, the upcoming and highly anticipated *Robin Hood: Prince of Thieves* offered promising but treacherous territory for yet another Hollywood remake. On the other hand, the subject matter had always been popular with Brits and Americans alike.

It seems remarkable that so many films have been made about Robin Hood, an historical figure who we're not sure even existed. To many he is just a medieval nursery story that has been exaggerated over the years, but that hasn't stopped him from being a favourite for film-makers. Five silent movies depicting his adventures had been made long before Douglas Fairbanks Sr got his hands on the role that made him a household name in 1922. Later, Errol Flynn's 1938 version did much the same for his career as it had done for Fairbanks's, while in the late '50s and early '60s the British-made *Robin Hood* television series established Richard Greene as the best and most familiar Robin Hood. Perhaps the greatest retelling of the Robin Hood story, however, came in 1976 when Sean Connery and Audrey Hepburn traded in youth for maturity to play *Robin and Marian* in the latter stages of their lives.

Watson and Densham's remake started out closer to the spirit of the original tale than anything else had before it, if only because, as Jerry Bruckheimer would do for his 2004 picture *King Arthur*, no one had done it that way before. Sure, they still wanted to surround Robin with all the familiar characters –Marian, Little John, Friar Tuck, the evil Sheriff of Nottingham – but they also wanted to bring Robin and his band of so-called outlaws into the twentieth century, adding some new characters, some fresh twists and turns, and a few surprises along the way.

One such surprise was the presentation of the crusades as the reason for King Richard's absence from England. There was even some discussion about the crusades' moral dubiety, which is even spelled out specifically several times to make sure the viewer understands that the English invasion of the Middle East was a fatal mistake. Indeed, Morgan Freeman's character, Azeem, certainly seems to show the superiority of Eastern technology and philosophy over Western culture. His frequent digs at the backwardness of the English make the underlying and largely unseen holy war easier for Christian audiences to stomach.

Feminism, too, seems to get a surprising boost in the form of Mary Elizabeth Mastrantonio's feisty and fully capable Maid Marian. Although Robin still comes to her rescue in the final battle sequence, she more than holds her own with a sword earlier on in the film and is every bit as headstrong and decisive as the title character himself.

More familiar to those acquainted with the 1984 *Robin of Sherwood* television series is Will Scarlet, Robin Hood's rebellious half-brother, played by Ray Winstone in the TV show as an angry, older character troubled by his wife's rape and murder. For the 1990s screenplay, however, the character of Scarlet – played by Christian – was rooted in jealousy. Christian made his first appearance in the film from behind the bushes on the perimeter of Sherwood Forest, shouting at Robin, 'Beg for mercy or die.' To some, his performance seemed so modern in his delivery that his character appears to have fallen out of some late-twentieth-century film like *Heathers* or *Pump Up the Volume* and into a time warp, being dropped into the twelfth century wholly unchanged.

Although Christian liked the character he was playing, he did agree that Watson and Densham had written Scarlet as a sort of twelfth-century James Dean: 'The script contained all these moments in which he was supposed to walk around, brooding, as James Dean would have done. I didn't like playing him that way and fought against it with director Kevin Reynolds. We wound up shooting a lot of different takes. My performance is all over the place, but it's up to Kevin to decide what he wants me to do in the finished film. Ultimately, I tried to avoid portraying Will as a hurt, angst-filled character who's insecure all the time. Especially in front of actors like Kevin Costner and Morgan Freeman. I didn't want to look like a weakling alongside them. Of course, none of this is to say that there's anything wrong with James Dean. The man was great. He was brilliant. But he can't be imitated.'

Certainly, continues Christian, 'several things were put into the script after I was cast – for instance, the fact that Robin Hood really screwed up my life when I was younger. His father dated my mother and I was the result. There is one point in the film when I have to tell Robin the truth. So it adds an edge to the whole movie for me. Will was obviously a bit of a wild child, too, and that comes over well. He had to grow up fast.' But there were still other elements of Christian's character about which he didn't see eye to eye with Reynolds, particularly the script's interpretation of Middle English speech. With lines likes 'Fuck me! He made it', it's hardly surprising.

However, Christian did find his costume more pleasing, and he was incredibly happy when the wardrobe people 'gave me rugged, beautifully layered leather stuff along with an extraordinarily large codpiece. They attached it to my costume, and I was very honoured. But, when people see that movie, they won't be watching me for a minute,' he jokes. 'Everybody's eyes will be on the codpiece.'

If Christian was assailed by self-doubt or intimidated when he worked alongside Sean Connery in *The Name of the Rose*, his work on *Robin Hood* gave him the opportunity to renew the acquaintance, as Connery appeared in a small cameo at the end of the film, playing King Richard at Robin and Marian's wedding. For some reason, though, Christian admits that he was 'terribly starstruck', a condition from which he suffers even today. 'I'm usually not very wordy when I meet somebody of great importance or talent. That's how it went with Morgan Freeman when I initially saw him on the set. Then I finally told myself, "Fuck it. Go up to the man." I walked over, introduced myself and said, "I think you're the greatest. I was raised with you. I used to watch you on *Sesame Street* all the time." Then he said, "Well thank you very much, but I was never on *Sesame Street*. It was *The Electric Company*." I was incredibly embarrassed, but he was sweet about it. He even wound up teaching me how to shoot bow and arrow so that I wouldn't look like a fool alongside all the other Merrie Men.' He laughs at the memory. 'I can't believe I'm in a movie with Merrie Men.'

Equally surprising was the choice of filming locations, none of which was in or around Nottingham, where the man of myth and legend was supposed to exist. Instead, the film was shot at a variety of locations that have nothing to do with Robin Hood whatsoever. For instance, the beach that was overlooked by gleaming white cliffs, for when Robin arrives home from the crusades, was the Seven Sisters, on the Sussex coast, west of Eastbourne, while several locations in Northumberland were commandeered for Robin's trek north to Nottingham. Wardour Castle in

Wiltshire was transformed into the ruin of Locksley Castle, Aysgarth Falls on the River Ure was used for where Robin fights Little John, and Robin's Sherwood Forest camp was built near Shepperton Film Studios, on whose back lot the square in Nottingham Castle was recreated. The interior shots of Nottingham Cathedral, meanwhile, were actually taken in a tiny church tucked away in Smithfield, London.

No doubt if Roger Ebert hears the rumour that a sequel is being planned, his response will probably be one of disbelief. He'll most likely be equally amused when he learns that Costner is looking to exploit the success of the original film by producing a big-screen spin-off that will catch up with the legendary character and his Merrie Men later on in life. *Robin Hood: Prince of Thieves 2*, Costner announced in February 2005, 'will be set several years after the first film, with the characters now evidently older. I am a little older, and I could take the whole story a stage further. [This] is an idea I am working on at the moment.'

When the original *Robin Hood: Prince of Thieves* opened, however, Christian was given precious little time to register any of the razzmatazz surrounding its premiere. In the same month, his next movie opened across America, albeit to a much smaller opening-weekend gross than *Prince of Thieves*.

Mobsters, as Roger Ebert noted in his review, is a strange movie to watch, largely because the four gangsters on whose life story the film is based were all in their early to mid-twenties. To the cinema-going public, a traditional gangster is one played by an actor like George Raft or Edward G Robinson, not Christian Slater or Patrick Dempsey.

Wittingly retitled around Hollywood as *The Godson* and *GoodlookingFellas*, the gangsters in *Mobsters* were half the age of Brando and De Niro and look in the film as if they're wearing their first decent suits and still learning to smoke without inhaling. But then, of course, all gangsters were presumably young once, including the four seminal figures in the movie: Lucky Luciano, Frank Costello, Meyer Lansky and Bugsy Siegel.

Mobsters traces the rise of these four gangsters from their youth on the streets of New York, during the years between the two world wars, to their gradual expansion from a small bootlegging business and thence to virtual control of the mob. What made their four-way partnership so special, in a criminal world dominated by Italians and Sicilians, was that two of them were Jewish, and all four had a greater loyalty to each other than to any of their other allies. Their nominal leader was Luciano, played by Christian, who is given the nickname 'Lucky' after an interesting little scene with Lansky (Patrick Dempsey), who has a guy tell a paperboy that a man in the back room has a job for him. The kid walks into the room, looks at Lansky and Luciano and instinctively picks Luciano, as he has the looks for the role. Indeed, Christian ages fairly convincingly here, playing a bad guy in his twenties or thirties.

The other two leading actors are Richard Grieco as Siegel and Costas Mandylor as Costello, and their mentors from the older generation of Hollywood are played by F Murray Abraham (gambler and fixer Arnold Rothstein), Anthony Quinn (a don named Masseria) and Michael Gambon (Masseria's arch-enemy, Don Faranzano). Meanwhile, Lara

Flynn Boyle of *Twin Peaks* has one of the few female roles, playing Lucky's girlfriend.

Overall, conceded Ebert, 'it is a good cast and they are in a well-made movie, but I was never really convinced. I admired the way the movie looked, all drenched in browns, golds and reds, and I liked the convincing sets and the art design. I believed the actors most of the time, too, which is a small miracle considering that I've seen so many of them so recently playing completely different and much younger characters. The problem is in the script, which is so complicated and violent that the credibility of the entire enterprise is undermined.'

Mobsters, continued Ebert, 'is about the bloody rise of its four heroes to the top of the crime establishment, by means so devious and labyrinthine that you almost have to take notes to figure out who's doing what, and why, and to whom. At one point, for example, having decided that the Quinn character must be killed, the four partners fake an attack on him, defend him, win his confidence by having saved his life, and then kill him. This is not the only double-reverse strategy in a movie which spends a good deal of the time with the characters explaining their strategy to each other, and to us.'

The body count in the movie is fairly high, but that's nothing compared to what's done to the bodies before they're counted in the bloodiest gangster movie Ebert could remember. Machine guns are emptied into dead bodies, a nose is bitten off, lips are cut off, a face is slowly and deliberately scarred, a man is dangled outside a hotel window before the rope is cut so he can fall to his death – and there are plenty of close-ups of faces and bodies after such things have happened to them. The violence and bloodshed are so far over the top, in fact, that – as Ebert notes – they do indeed undermine the rest of the film, approaching parody.

Mobsters pretends to be a sociological study of the management levels of the mob, but it's as blood-soaked as any violent action picture (there's more mayhem in it, for example, than in Jean-Claude Van Damme's *Double Impact*, even though Van Damme is sold exclusively on his body counts). What survives, concludes Ebert, beyond 'the gunfire and the screaming are some nice small moments in which the gangsters use intelligence to try to reason their way through the anarchy of the mob's operational methods. Much is made of the fact that ethnic rivalries have been buried, that Jews and Italians are co-operating here for mutual benefit, that a character like Lansky always prefers to substitute negotiation for murder. When the movie slows down and takes a breath for these scenes, they work nicely and are well acted, but too often the general noise level obscures the movie's real achievements.'

At around the time of the film's release, Christian confessed that, if he had to choose the person whose life he would prefer to live, it would be Lucky Luciano's: 'Not because he was a cold-blooded killer or anything, but because I like his control and intelligence. He was calm, cool and quiet – until somebody pushed his buttons. Then he became a totally ruthless man. Completely brutal. When he wanted to get back at somebody, he always did it, regardless of how long it took. You know – sweet, sweet revenge. It's the greatest.' Above all, Christian continues (and perhaps this is where he became fascinated with the role), 'Lucky began to hold all the cards in organised crime. He didn't take any shit and pushed his way right to the top, no matter what the cost. He was a hard-edged character. He couldn't be bought or sold, and he didn't want to be screwed over. I feel that way a bit about myself. I don't want to sell out or do anything silly like that, so there are some similarities between us. And Luciano was also very loyal. If killing a friend would get him on somebody's good side, Luciano wouldn't do it, even if it meant risking his own life.'

However, Christian was also determined to show a more sympathetic side of the extremely violent character he was playing. 'He definitely faces quite a few moral dilemmas, because, with him, it's not just feelings getting hurt, it's people getting killed, and it hurt Luciano when somebody close to him got taken out. But if a guy he disliked pissed him off just slightly, he'd make Frank or Bugsy kill the son of a bitch. After a while, though, once they started fucking up, he began doing the killings himself. But our movie doesn't cover that period.'

Anyone who thought that Christian had taken on the roles of Lucky Luciano and Will Scarlet in a calculated effort to make a break from teen films would probably be mistaken, because he's never had much of a career plan. 'The choices that I truly made for myself were *Heathers* and *Pump Up the Volume*, two movies that everybody advised me against doing. I loved those scripts and did everything I could to ensure being cast in them. Films like *Robin Hood* and *Mobsters*, on the other hand, were attractive projects because of the people involved in them.'

Chapter 6

You're So Cool

In his heart of hearts, Christian has always been a trekkie. Obsessed with the *Star Trek* television series, it's said that his permanently arched eyebrows stem from a misguided attempt to mimic Leonard Nimoy's Mr Spock one Halloween, so one can only imagine the excitement and joy he must have felt when his mother nabbed him a cameo role of communications officer on the starship *Excelsior* in 1991's penultimate big-screen outing for Captain Kirk in *Star Trek VI: The Undiscovered Country*. He literally loved the idea of being on set with his all-time hero William Shatner, and was so thrilled to be part of the film that, rather than spend the $750 cheque he was paid, he framed it.

Three years later, when he was on the Paramount lot, in his trailer, after watching his favourite episode of *Star Trek: The Next Generation*, he decided to walk over to the *Star Trek* set and introduce himself to Patrick Stewart, shake his hand

and take his seat. 'I sat in the captain's chair,' he told *Premiere* magazine editor Veronica Chambers, smiling at the memory. 'Stewart took pictures of me. It was one of those rare moments when I enjoy being me. I wasn't just some nut off the street; I was Christian Slater.'

When *Interview* magazine caught up with him for a 1991 feature, however, he had just completed *Kuffs*, his third movie in a year and another that his mother, Mary Jo, hadn't wanted him to make. But Christian loved the idea of recreating the sassy talk-to-camera style that had successfully launched Matthew Broderick in *Ferris Bueller's Day Off*. Of course, in that movie, the idea of talking to the camera worked a treat, but not in *Kuffs* – perhaps unsurprisingly, considering its $21 million box office.

The film, said Christian at the time, 'centres on my character, a young guy who inherits a business after his brother gets killed on the job. He becomes the head of a protection agency that patrols a section of San Francisco and keeps an eye on its clients' businesses. At the beginning of the film, my character is dodging every responsibility he can, and by the end he realises that there are certain choices you have to make. Sometimes you have to put your feelings behind you and think about other people. The film has a lot of messages in it, and there are plenty of similarities to my own life.'

If one of these was the period when he was drinking heavily, he was able to explain away his behaviour with comparative ease. 'I did what a lot of people do at a certain age. I went through a wild period, although I think I took it to an extreme and I know I could have been smarter. There were a few relationships that could have gone better, some situations that might have swung my way, but I don't regret my past. I actually learned from the negative experiences. They taught me that I don't want to get up in the morning and wonder whether I should be embarrassed about what I did the night before. I got tired of being my own worst enemy and found out that there's nothing positive about self-destruction. I definitely would not be so heavily involved in *Kuffs* if I was still living that way.'

Kuffs was released at the beginning of 1992 in America and rapidly became a critical and box-office disappointment. Richard Harrington, writing in the *Washington Post*, branded it as 'krap', and maybe he was right. As he pointed out, because the film could never decide 'whether it's playing for laughs or for keeps, it stumbles and falls flat on its face. Worse, it must rely on the charms of Christian Slater to carry a preposterous plot. Slater, who has successfully portrayed quirky, rebellious outsiders with maniac streaks in *Heathers* and *Pump Up the Volume*, never gets a handle here, and the film-makers have further saddled him with the hoariest of tricks: Slater talks to the camera, wisecracking, explaining plot loopholes and finessing loopy plot-holes. Essentially, he's asides himself.

'Slater plays George Kuffs,' Harrington continues, 'a never-done-well twenty-one-year-old who abandons his pregnant girlfriend (the vacuously lovely Milla Jovovich) and ends up in San Francisco, where he tries to put the bite on big brother Bruce Boxleitner. Boxleitner is head of one of the city's Patrol Specials, organised adjuncts to the police department dating back to the last century. Unfortunately, big brother is gunned down in a church and Slater suddenly inherits the policing business. Soon, he must juggle his desire to wreak revenge on his brother's killer and his need to work with the police to keep the business alive.

'Not that anyone's going to care. There's so little right with this film that it never engages a viewer, except sporadically or accidentally. Police liaison Tony Goldwyn, a gregarious accident waiting to happen, is the funniest thing about *Kuffs*. As for Slater, even conceding that he's been given little to work with, it's quite apparent that he's worn out his welcome. He's not convincing as either a cad or a cop. The appropriate script line: "I'm history, that's what I think."'

The most offensive thing about *Kuffs*, concluded Harrington, 'is not its lack of substance or absence of achievement but its PG-13 rating, suggesting it is suitable for children. That rating and the previews highlight the movie's zany and perhaps edgy aspects but do not at all suggest its level of violence. The rating means *Kuffs* contains material that may be inappropriate for children under 13 but is open to anyone, with or without an adult escort.' In Dallas, strangely enough, the city's ratings board added a warning that the movie's content was 'suitable, except for drugs, violence and language', suggesting that nudity is the only no-no for kids.

With another cameo lined up in *Where The Day Takes You* (this time as an uncredited social worker) and a role as the voice of Pips in the animated *FernGully: The Last Rain Forest*, many were asking why Christian had no film in which he had a starring role or why he didn't have a hit that he could call his own. With the exception of *Young Guns II* and *Robin Hood: Prince of Thieves*, none of his films had grossed more than $30 million at the box office, and the career that was supposed to have taken off had yet to leave the runway.

There seemed to be no shortage of critics who were quick to compare Christian's career to that of his *Heathers* co-star Winona Ryder. As *Premiere* magazine correctly noted, she had worked with such directors as Martin Scorsese, Tim Burton and Jim Jarmusch, while, in the same period of time, Christian hadn't worked with one director who had even been nominated for an Academy Award. But the magazine still believed he had a good chance of capturing the first-rank stardom that had been predicted for him. If it was true that Hollywood hadn't been able to find a fully bankable male star in his twenties since Tom Cruise was unleashed in 1983's *Risky Business*, it wasn't from the lack of trying. The problem was that even the most promising candidates couldn't – or wouldn't – fit the bill. Charlie Sheen foundered in the romance genre, Johnny Depp proudly resisted attempts to put him in formula action pictures, John Cusack wasn't working often enough, and it seemed that Brad Pitt and Keanu Reeves were the only current young actors who could carry a gun, get the girl and tell a joke.

Then again, at the time Christian was only just hitting his mid-twenties. 'That's what a lot of people don't realise,' defended Dan Lauria at the time. 'He's five or six years behind guys like Cruise and Pitt. I don't think anyone's seen the best of Christian yet. As he gets more comfortable with characterisations, and as people allow him to step away from his image, they'll begin to see what he's capable of.'

Even if the critics were right – that *Kuffs* was a bad movie and that Christian had lost the sparkle from his performance – his next film would improve things dramatically. Not that he would be very enthusiastic about the project. In fact, recalls director Tony Bill, 'I had to drag him kicking and screaming into it. I told him, "The reason you're afraid to do this is because there's no character to hide behind, no glib, snappy dialogue, no costume, no gun," and that's hard to trust as an actor. I told him I was going to make him the opposite of what he'd done in all his other movies. He's considerably more multifaceted than the roles he'd chosen in the past, and I wasn't going to let him be a clown or a smartass; I was going after simplicity and honesty. Above all, I told him that he could open up his career and be taken seriously as a dramatic actor, not a teen idol or a smart kid.'

Although *Untamed Heart* only made $19 million at the US box office, its comparatively low production budget of $7 million meant that it hardly qualified it as a failure. More importantly, of course, it proved to critics and to Hollywood that Christian wasn't, as *Premiere* magazine put it, 'just another young actor, kinetic on hormonal adrenaline'.

Although Christian was initially reluctant, in the end he was pleased that he'd accepted the role. 'In other parts I've had to be very boisterous, which is nothing like this role. It was threatening at first because the character of Adam is actually more like the real me: quiet and reserved. He grew up in an orphanage and spent a large part of his life alone, so he doesn't easily relate to people. And the story that the nuns told him about how his parents died makes him feel special, but set apart. He feels different and alone … I feel more comfortable if people have the image of me from this movie. It's a much easier image to live up to: sweet guy, down-to-earth and gentle.'

An early publicity picture of Christian from 1988.

Christian's big-screen deflowering with Chilean actress, Valentina Vargas, in *The Name of The Rose* was one of the most unexpectedly erotic moments of 1980s cinema.

Above: As Jason 'JD' Dean in *Heathers*, Christian was elevated into a fully-fledged movie star, even though the film could hardly be called a box-office smash.

Below: Christian with his *Heathers* co-star, Winona Ryder, at the Oscars Governors Ball in Los Angeles in 1989. The couple became romantically involved during the making of the film.

Above left: Like *Heathers*, Christian as DJ, Happy Harry Hard-On, in *Pump Up The Volume* was another movie that Christian was warned off making.

Above right: Christian as Kevin Costner's half-brother, Will Scarlett, in *Robin Hood: Prince of Thieves* remains to this day Christian's most successful movie.

Below: With co-star Marisa Tomei in *Untamed Heart*, released in 1993. A role Christian was initially reluctant to accept.

Above left: With girlfriend Nina Huang at the premiere of *Dave* at Mann's National Theatre in Los Angeles, 1993.

Above right: Patricia Arquette was another of Christian's co-stars to become romantically involved with him during the making of *True Romance* in 1993.

Below: A publicity shot for *True Romance*. *From left to right,* Val Kilmer, Bronson Pinchot, Christian, Christopher Penn, Patricia Arquette and Dennis Hopper.

The now famous mug shot of Christian after he was arrested at New York's John F. Kennedy Airport in December 1994, for packing a gun into his holdall and trying to board an aircraft.

Above: Christian was reunited with Samantha Mathis for *Broken Arrow*, five years after they had worked together and fallen in love on the set of 1990's *Pump Up The Volume*.

Below left: Poster artwork for *Broken Arrow* featured images of John Travolta and Christian as the headlining stars.

Below right: Christian at the premiere of *Hard Rain* in Los Angeles, 1998. The next day he started a ninety day prison sentence.

Although Christian was rumoured to have been dating former girlfriend Kim Walker
at the time, he attended the November 1988 premiere of *Very Bad Things* with co-star,
Cameron Diaz.

Once he'd accepted it, Christian researched the role by repeatedly watching kinescopes of Jack Palance in a Playhouse 90 production of *Requiem for a Heavyweight*. Playing a painfully shy and withdrawn character kept him in control, Christian said at the time. 'It made for an interesting life lesson for me. I found that, when I'm calm and at peace, I can really have a great time. There wasn't a lot of the malarkey that usually goes on, on the set. Everything seemed to be really, really simple.'

Untamed Heart is, in essence, a working-class love story. Caroline (Marisa Tomei) is an outgoing, ambitious and street-smart waitress on the all-night shift at a Minneapolis diner, while Adam (Christian) is a gentle misfit who works in the diner's kitchen and never seems to have anything to say. The film describes how Adam was raised by nuns in an orphanage and has a weak heart – so weak, in fact, that he sometimes lost consciousness on the playground at school. An operation left a scar running across his chest, but as the film moves up to the present it is revealed that he needs a heart transplant, and he needs it urgently. The problem is that he doesn't want one because he was told a story by the nuns about being raised in the jungle and being given the heart of a great ape, which makes him ferocious and strong. He lives by himself, reads a lot, washes dishes and doesn't talk – except to Caroline, who breaks through his reserve when she bandages a cut on his hand.

As film critic Roger Ebert notes in his review, 'Tony Bill's direction walks a thin line between the fable of the underlying story and the realism of the world the characters live in. For instance, when Caroline walks home late one night through the park, she is attacked by would-be rapists and is rescued by Adam, who has been furtively following her home each evening to make sure she arrives safely. But he is much too timid to tell her how he feels. When she discovers his story, and their romance blossoms, tenderly and tentatively, the movie moves into what most critics described as sweet and kind of goofy, and works, because its heart is in the right place and because Marisa and Christian undoubtedly project the right note of mystery into the ultimately doomed romance.'

Adding to the appeal was a sprinkling of salt-of-the-earth supporting characters, of whom a favourite was Rosie Perez, playing Caroline's fellow waitress and best friend. Although Perez essentially played the same character that she portrayed so well in *White Men Can't Jump*, she has less to do in *Untamed Heart*. She smokes a lot, but then so does almost everyone else in the movie. But that criticism – if it was one – didn't seem to worry director and producer Tony Bill in the slightest; if anything, he took pains to enthusiastically explain his attraction to the movie. 'I like scripts that are original in both concept and execution, and populated with people you haven't met before. This story wasn't a clone of other movies, and it encompassed a spectrum of emotional colour, from funny to crazy to sad.'

Co-producer Helen Bartlett agreed: 'This is not a big action picture; it is much more character-driven. It is a true love story – emotional and moving – and has all the qualities of a great Hollywood movie, without the special effects.'

The script, strangely enough, was discovered during one of Tony Bill's renowned talent hunts. 'I'm always on the lookout for talent I've never heard of, so I'd asked an agent at William Morris to send over some scripts from new writers,' he recalls. It was in this haphazard fashion that he discovered Tom Sierchio's noteworthy script. 'It had been originally submitted, two weeks earlier, only as a writer's sample, but I loved it for its own values.' What both Bill and Bartlett also loved was the story's theme of 'having someone, somebody you never would have expected, come into your life and really transform you, change you'.

If finding the script seemed straightforward, casting the two main characters didn't prove so simple. It was clear from the start that the actor cast in the pivotal role of Adam would have a challenging task in conveying so much feeling with so little dialogue. Perhaps Christian was considered an odd choice for the role, which was, after all, a far cry from any of his previous parts, but Bill wasn't concerned. 'When his name was mentioned, it was a surprise, but then it became the obvious choice.'

The casting of Marisa Tomei as Caroline was also a key factor to the movie's success. Once again, Bill was after an actress who could capture the character's combination of vulnerability and strength. Perhaps it was Marisa's success in 1992's *My Cousin Vinny* that convinced Bill she was the correct choice. After reading the script, she had no hesitation in accepting the role. 'It just hit my heart,' she remembers. But what she liked most about the film was how it looked at things from Caroline's perspective. 'The story is about letting go of her picture of who she is supposed to be with, and falling in love with the right person, who just happens to have been right under her nose. Caroline is insecure and really hadn't taken risks in her life, but when she finally decides to take a chance, she gets this wonderful gift in Adam.' The interplay between Marisa and Christian proved to be a marvellous combination.

Another major asset for the film was being able to shoot in Minneapolis itself. For instance, Jim's Diner, which acts as the centrepiece of the story in the movie, was actually a real-life restaurant called Jim's Diner. 'It's as real as it would be if we'd come here to shoot a documentary about Jim's,' Bill reflected. 'It has a wonderful combination of ingredients from every diner you've ever been to. We've done very little to change it for the film. In fact, we changed the original name of the diner in the script to reflect that it *is* Jim's. The diner is where real life begins in this movie. It's a place where people come together, so it's sort of the spawning ground of our story.'

Certainly, when shooting began in March 1992, winter was still very much in evidence, which was perfect for the setting of the story. And perhaps what surprised the cast and crew was the number of local residents who turned out to watch the filming, braving temperatures dipping as low as seventeen degrees below zero.

Filming two months later, however, was not so straightforward. By then the temperature had risen and so the set designers had to resort to spraying fake snow on the sidewalks and in the trees. And, when several young admirers took it upon themselves to track down where Christian was staying, he had to be secretly moved in the middle of the night to another residence. Of course, this didn't bother Christian one bit; he always greeted his fans, no matter what, and on more than one occasion he purposely stepped outside his trailer in downpours specifically to sign autographs and talk with those who had been waiting in the rain for a glimpse of him.

Essentially, however, the shoot went according to plan and, as far as Christian was concerned, his life 'couldn't have been better' during filming. Perhaps one of the reasons why he was feeling so good was the prospect of his next movie project, a movie with the title *True Romance*.

'I begged him not to do it,' remembers Dan Lauria. Christian, however, was convinced that there was every good reason to accept. First, he reasoned, it was written by Quentin Tarantino, the guy who'd written *Reservoir Dogs*, and, second, the new project gave him the chance to work with some great actors. 'Doing what?' Lauria had asked. 'Dennis Hopper's the only one you have any dialogue with. All the rest of them are just screaming, yelling and shooting. That's not acting.'

Despite Lauria's counsel and misgivings, Christian did the movie anyway. He had, after all, been advised against making *Heathers* and *Pump Up the Volume*, and they were the movies that established him as a name to be reckoned with. And now, as then, his refusal to listen to advice was completely right.

Christian remembers that the script for *True Romance* hit him from the moment he read it. 'I saw this great, great dialogue and a chance to play a really interesting guy who shows a lot of colours and emotions. He is someone who definitely is not the norm, to say the least. I would say this is one of those true "live fast, die young, leave a good-looking corpse" movies.'

As it turned out, however, 'with all the expectations I had of that film, it was one of the hugest letdowns I've ever had in my entire career,' admitted Christian. 'But I still think it's a great movie.'

Even if the results did fail to set the box office alight, and even if he did have to stand by as others basked in the glow of Tarantino's *Pulp Fiction* twelve months later, it still became a personal favourite among Christian's own performances and – even better – a personal favourite of the critics.

In the movie, Christian played Clarence Worley, a loner who works in a comic-book store and spends most of his spare hours watching old kung-fu movies and idolising Elvis Presley. With no girl and very little romance in his life, he is spending his birthday alone at a Sonny Chiba kung-fu triple bill in a small seedy theatre when he is suddenly joined by Alabama Whitman (Patricia Arquette), who spills her popcorn on him, on purpose, while finding her seat in the movie house. What Clarence doesn't know is that she is a call girl hired by his boss as a birthday favour. Their instant passion for each other leads them to quick marriage and a series of wildly improbable events in their search for happiness.

When Clarence discovers the truth about Alabama's past, he becomes very protective, killing her former employer, a horrifying pimp played by Gary Oldman. When he returns, however, Clarence is stunned to discover that a suitcase he thought was full of her belongings is actually full of cocaine. This development leads to the heart of the story, which is of two young lovers on the run from the mob, who want their cocaine back. After Clarence becomes reunited with his estranged father, Clifford (Dennis Hopper), he and Alabama head for California to sell the cocaine and live happily ever after. Their contact in Los Angeles is Dick Ritchie (Mark Rapaport), a struggling actor who has some connections and might be able to help sell the drugs.

Dick knows of a producer named Lee Donowitz (Saul Rubinek) who can come up with the cash for the cocaine, but first Dick and Clarence must convince him that there's no risk in the deal. As Lee's assistant, Elliot Blitzer (Bronson Pinchot), reveals, the big-time movie producer has sellers who are reliable and safe. However, Lee would prefer to be cautious about committing to buy the drugs from a no-name kid like Clarence. Unfortunately, Elliot isn't very discreet about the potential deal and, after a patrolman pulls him over, under the influence and covered with cocaine, an investigation ensues and hotshot cops Nicky Dimes (Chris Penn) and Cody Nicholson (Tom Sizemore) grow excited over the possibility of busting one of Hollywood's leading producers.

Now, with both the mob and the LAPD after them, Clarence and Alabama's situation grows increasingly complicated. The fact that they don't know about their pursuers adds tension to their predicament. Sure, they know what they are doing is illegal, but with Tarantino's gift for creating sympathy for criminals, the audience is drawn in to simply wishing the very best for the lovebirds and hope that, somehow, they can get away unscathed and with their dreams coming true and intact.

True Romance is divided neatly into three acts, each of which ends in an act of violence. The first ends with Vincenzo Coccotti (Christopher Walken) paying a visit to Clifford Worley in an effort to track down Clarence and, although Clifford doesn't co-operate, what follows is perhaps one of the finest moments in the movie. But, of course, Vincenzo is an intellectual man who listens with interest, humour and increasing rage as Clifford explains the origins of Sicilians, using language as a weapon with which to wound his assailants. The second act ends with Coccotti's henchman Virgil (James Gandolfini) attacking Alabama in her motel room, in a bloody fight that is unflinching in its brutality. The third and final act is one of those that Tarantino loves best, with all involved parties in the same room, pointing guns at each other, and, in the middle of the confusion, the film's main characters – in this case, Clarence and Alabama.

True Romance was released in America in September 1993 and, according to *Rolling Stone*, everything about it was dynamite. The movie allowed Christian and Arquette to 'make a wildly comic and sexy pair of bruised romantics' and everyone else to shine 'right down to the smallest bits from Brad Pitt as a stoned innocent to Val Kilmer as the ghost of Elvis. But it's Tarantino's gutter poetry that detonated the film.'

Roger Ebert, in his review, also observed that 'the energy and style of the movie are exhilarating. Christian Slater has the kind of cocky recklessness the movie needs, and Patricia Arquette portrays a fetching combination of bimbo and best pal'. A lot of that could probably be put down to Tony Scott's direction, simply because the movie featured familiar passages of action and violence. But, cautions Scott, to fixate on the violence is to miss the point. 'There are two sides to the film. It is a bittersweet movie. I had actors such as

Christian and Patricia who have charm as well as a darker side that suits the story well. Violence is integral to the piece but it is not gratuitous. It is the nature of the beast. I wanted to show that, although true romance can survive, it does so in a very dangerous world.'

Certainly filming Tarantino's vibrant screenplay – the first the writer had ever written and sold – brought a new challenge to Scott. 'This movie shoots from the hip and creates a fascinating mixture of several elements. It's a love story, an action piece and a chase film that affords a brilliant ensemble of actors an extraordinary chance to shine.'

Once Christian and Patricia were on board, the casting snowballed from there, with a number of leading actors attracted to relatively small parts. The aforementioned Gary Oldman signed on as the repulsive pimp Drexl, a white drug trader who sports dreadlocks and flawlessly mimics black street talk. 'He's a nasty piece of work,' explained Oldman, whose past credits include biopics as disparate as *Sid and Nancy* and *JFK*, as well as *Bram Stoker's Dracula*, in which he appeared alongside Christian's *Heathers* co-star Winona Ryder. 'I found the voice I wanted for him while filming in Queens on *Romeo Is Bleeding*,' continues Oldman about his character. 'We were in this very dodgy neighbourhood at night and I heard this guy, who was black, talking outside my trailer, so I invited him in and recorded him on my tape player. He was my vocal role model.'

Christopher Walken, meanwhile, was attracted to what he described as the screenplay's almost theatrical quality. 'Quentin writes big pieces of dialogue, almost like a play. I've spent a lot of my life doing plays and working with big chunks of dialogue. You don't see those chunks in movies often. The complexity and amount of information that is conveyed through them here is practically Elizabethan drama.'

Dennis Hopper, recruited to play Christian's father, agreed: 'I liked the fact that it was a character-driven drama. The motivating force of any piece is the people within it. This is wonderfully written, in that, even though I have a smaller part, that part is complete within itself, with points of comedy and drama. The whole script is acutely real and honest.'

True Romance was yet another movie in which Christian became romantically involved with his co-star while shooting, even if only for a short time. During the making of the film, Christian remembers, 'We got very close. It's one of those unavoidable things.' The protracted nude love scene they had together was, Christian says, 'really special. I lost sight of the crew being around. It was the first time nothing on the outside really mattered.' But, then, with her expressive blue eyes, soft Southern-tinged voice, and an acting range that can carry her from hysterically funny to terrifying in seconds, it perhaps shouldn't be too surprising that Patricia and Christian would end up in a relationship, even it was a brief encounter.

Perhaps the character Patricia was playing helped. 'Alabama has had a more difficult life than most,' she observed, 'but she's a romantic at heart. She also knows how to defend herself and fight for what she loves, even if that means dying for her man.'

Interestingly enough, Patricia and Christian both went through major changes in appearance in order to play their roles. Christian had his normally light-brown, longish hair cut spike-short and coloured jet black, while Patricia's long, sandy-brown hair was cut into a short '70s bob with butterfly waves dyed platinum blonde.

In the same month that *True Romance* was playing across American screens, Christian invited journalist Todd Gold to tour the downstairs of his three-bedroom Spanish-style house in Los Angeles, where the reporter would unearth Christian's most prized possessions. 'Over here is the *Batman* memorabilia,' wrote Gold later, 'and over there is the stuff from *Star Trek*, including, on the wall, a framed shirt once worn by Captain Kirk. The sacred garment, signed by Trek star William Shatner, right up there with his 1961 Cadillac and his new Porsche – and considering his reputation as a smouldering, stubble-faced gangster of love in *Romance*, that is perhaps slightly surprising.'

But, Gold wondered, was this really what Christian was into? Didn't the winner of the MTV Movie Award for Most Desirable Male have any pastimes that weren't quite so nerdy? Christian considered the question and then let loose one of his patented leers. 'Just the usual,' he replied. 'Sex toys.'

More than anything else, Christian loves to play. Although he is still, to this day, deadly serious about his movie career and has been ever since he made his film debut at the age of fifteen as a boy on the run from a murder rap in the 1985 film *The Legend of Billie Jean*, he brings to each project what director Allan Moyle calls 'a built-in glee factor'. Todd Gold explains, 'His characters may be morally messy rebels, but they smile a lot, and their eyes flicker with mystery and mischief. A generation of young female filmgoers are under his spell.'

Christian is, in a word, cool. And he's way beyond caring that *Cosmopolitan* once named him Hollywood's Most Promising Male Star. 'They vote you Greatest Kisser, Biggest Muscles. I try to distance myself from all that malarkey.' Even his mother, Mary Jo, doesn't quite understand what the commotion is about: 'Sometimes I look at him and think, They're making such a fuss over my little boy. Somebody tell me why.'

In his 1993 *People Weekly* article, Gold perhaps found the best way to describe Christian's attitude at the time: 'Give him a chance to do battle with the bottle and he will lose bigtime but live to tell the tale. Cast him opposite a beautiful woman and he could very well fall in love. He is vulnerable; he is a man of action; and he is desirous of spaghetti and meatballs.'

Indeed, Patricia Arquette could hardly stand it. As her character says to Christian's at a pivotal point in the surprisingly touching story of two young losers lugging a suitcase full of cocaine and fleeing the law and the mob, 'You're so cool.'

She was right. Christian had never been more in sync with a movie persona than he was with Clarence Worley, the crazy-yet-lovable comic-book-store clerk he plays in *True Romance*, a movie already flush with weirdos, including Brad Pitt as the ultimate drug-hazed loafer. Screenwriter Quentin Tarantino remembers thinking, when he first met Christian, how the young actor was 'this knockaround, goofy kid, with a real sweet side he keeps hidden'.

With such personal praise and a critically acclaimed performance now behind him, it seemed only natural that Christian would accept a supporting role in director Barry Levinson's forthcoming project, a movie that, even in pre-production, promised to be a departure in setting, style and budget.

Chapter 7

Hollywood Hell

By 1993, Christian's agent, Rick Kurtzman at CAA, his mother, Mary Jo, and his publicist, Susan Culley, all seemed determined that Christian should make the kind of movie that would make him into a fully fledged movie star. And so did he.

Although there were those who were slightly baffled when he took on the role of a dim-witted, streetwise videotape-head in Barry Levinson's *Jimmy Hollywood*, Christian, and all those around him, had their reasons to believe that it was a good springboard with which to elevate Christian out of the roles he had been used to playing in the past and, hopefully, help to establish him as a genuine star. All the same, it was a role for which, outside of his own circle of colleagues, he would perhaps have been considered an odd choice. But, as Christian himself pointed out at the time, all that mattered was 'the quality of the project and the people

I'm making a strong attempt to work with and have relationships with'. Besides, he continued, 'I've gotten to a place in my life where I don't need to play the wild and crazy guy. I can play an actual human being and, all in all, *Jimmy Hollywood* worked out beautifully. It's giving me a nice pacing and feeling to my career. It just doesn't feel as chaotic as it did that one year when I did all those friggin' movies back to back and lost my mind.'

Whatever the criticisms surrounding his choice of casting Christian, director Levinson wasn't concerned, noting that, 'For a younger guy who's got a certain degree of success, Christian seems to really want to be there to work.' The only trouble was, Levinson was on the rebound from the expensive and embarrassing flop *Toys* and, although it all looked promising on paper, *Jimmy Hollywood* wasn't necessarily the correct answer for what either Christian or Levinson wanted to achieve. Less expensive and less embarrassing than Levinson's previous project, it was, according to Peter Travers, writing in *Rolling Stone* magazine, still 'a clinker'.

'*Jimmy Hollywood* was meant to be the film that let Levinson move fast on his feet again,' Travers continued in his review, 'with none of the studied myth-making that infected his family saga *Avalon*. Working with dispatch on TV's *Homicide* inspired him to shoot *Jimmy Hollywood* in Los Angeles in just six weeks for a relatively low budget of $16 million. The plot seemed simple: Jimmy Alto, played by a newly blond Joe Pesci, is an actor from New Jersey who's determined to make Hollywood beg for his talent. So far, there are no takers. His hairdresser girlfriend, Lorraine De

La Peña (Spain's vivacious Victoria Abril), longs to groom the rich and famous. Christian plays William, an idiot savant who knows electronics and nothing else but will follow Jimmy anywhere.

'These are the Hollywood fringes, and Levinson knows them well. He arrived there from Baltimore in the 1970s, seeking work as an actor, writer and comedian. For a while, there's *Diner*-like humour and feeling in Jimmy's musings on fame as he and William stroll the walk of stars on the depressingly seedy Hollywood Boulevard.

'But Levinson can't or won't stay simple. He grabs a big issue – crime – and runs with it. Jimmy needs an outlet for his career frustrations so he becomes a vigilante. It's a great role. With William's help, he makes videos of dealers and thieves in the act and sends the tapes to TV stations. The police are humiliated, but Jimmy's a saviour of the streets, a star. But there's a catch: revealing his identity could get him killed. Levinson pumps up the link between crime and celebrity as if he'd just discovered the hackneyed theme. Along the way, what could have been a minor movie gem comes apart at the seams.'

Released in America in March 1994, *Jimmy Hollywood* was a particularly personal movie for Levinson. As producer Mark Johnson noted, 'Hollywood has very strong emotional ties for him, and this one really got us back to the source, to what is really most fun about making movies. There's something about lower-budget films that is so satisfying. It's just as imaginative, but you have to be even more resourceful.'

It's interesting to note from the production notes that, on his arrival in Hollywood, Levinson attended acting school, shared an $80-per-month studio apartment off Hollywood Boulevard with two friends, and worked in a deli. In fact, the character of Jimmy Alto in the movie, and his absurd tribulations as a deli waiter, were directly taken from Levinson's personal experience, as is his fascination with Hollywood as it was.

Hollywood as it is – frenetic, graffitied, simmering – figures prominently in Levinson's rough-hewn perspective on the state of contemporary urban hope, but in *Jimmy Hollywood* Levinson's Hollywood is a place where everything has deteriorated, except the aspirations that made it in the first place. 'Hollywood is more dangerous and volatile than it was before, with an on-the-surface, explosive danger,' Levinson says. 'Jimmy represents those who are frustrated and on the edge, yet in comedic sensibility. Ultimately, the mythology of Hollywood also pertains to [the United States], to every troubled city where many dreams have died or are dying. And yet, that belief still exists in people: that they can accomplish and ultimately succeed. It's a fascinating contradiction.'

It's pretty much the same view expressed by journalist and author Christopher Wilson in his 1999 biography of Goldie Hawn. 'Hollywood is hard town. Neither forgiving nor forgetting, it stands by and watches you fall. Unless you have some hidden resolve, some inner steel, you will not survive there long, be you shoeshine boy or superstar. In Hollywood the road to success can be short, but it is a narrow highway, one where accidents occur. To stay on the road and to move forward is a virtual impossibility.'

Central to *Jimmy Hollywood* is Joe Pesci's performance of a would-be actor who literally can't even get arrested in Hollywood. 'I love the character,' said Pesci. 'Jimmy is from back East and comes from the street. He has tremendous faith in himself and his talent. I can relate to the character. Trying to get ahead is just impossible. I've been acting since I was five, but coming to Hollywood, there are all the frustrations of trying to get in. You just have to be lucky.'

In contrast, Christian observes that his character, William, is 'a little vague and may be extremely slow, but there are definitely thoughts going on in his head. William is not a judgemental person. He's just a very simple guy who follows Jimmy around and listens to all the crazy stories he tells him, and spends a lot of time in his own little world.'

Certainly, that's how Pesci explained the unusual bond of friendship between the two characters: 'Jimmy likes the way William is, and William likes the way Jimmy is. Jimmy can talk to William and bounce ideas off him. In turn, Jimmy tries to help him in certain ways and teach him things.' In many ways, the two men's relationship is similar to that between the characters played by Tom Cruise and Dustin Hoffman in Levinson's Oscar-winning 1988 movie *Rain Man*. Critic Roger Ebert considered this aspect of the film its most commendable trait, that 'in Pesci and Slater, Levinson has actors who find the right tone for the material, although the plot weighs them down'.

But what Ebert particularly liked was the 'wonderful opening shot in which Jimmy Alto, would-be actor, walks down Hollywood Boulevard reciting the name on every star on the pavement, by memory. There are people who can do this. And there are a lot of people like Jimmy holding on desperately to the leftover dreams of many years ago, still hoping to be discovered.'

The principal photography for *Jimmy Hollywood* began on 4 August 1993 and, like a tour of Hollywood mythology, the production made stops at the Hollywood Boulevard Walk of Fame, the Hollywood Bowl (where The Beatles played their famous concert in August 1964) and the El Capitan and Egyptian theatres, as well as places the tour buses don't visit (especially after dark) and other sites that manifest how Hollywood evolved.

Whether or not *Jimmy Hollywood* was a box-office smash or not, six months before the movie went into production another title was already stealing the limelight from its competitors. The November 1992 release of Francis Ford Coppola's *Bram Stoker's Dracula* enjoyed both the biggest opening in Columbia Pictures' history and the biggest non-summertime opening in Hollywood history.

At the time, of course, many asked, why do a remake of *Dracula*? It was, after all, based on a story that had been told a hundred times before. At this time, vampires were coming back in vogue, in both print (Anne Rice was at the time approaching the fourth instalment of her bestselling *Vampire Chronicles*) and film, with some half-dozen vampire movies already either in or approaching production, ranging from the popular (i.e. *Buffy, the Vampire Slayer*) to the lewd (i.e. Roger Corman's *To Sleep with a Vampire*). Indeed, there would soon be a legendary adaptation of Rice's *Interview with the Vampire*, which to many was arguably the most celebrated work of vampire fiction since Bram Stoker's *Dracula* was first published in 1897. In fact, the *Washington Post* literary critic called the adaptation of Rice's cult novel 'a thrilling, strikingly original work of the imagination. Sometimes horrible, sometimes beautiful, always unforgettable.' No question about it, vampires were hot, and in retrospect it should be no surprise that the idea of making a film out of the novel had been doing the Hollywood rounds since the end of the '70s, the decade in which it was published. So popular was it, in fact, that it had even been considered, at one time, for a television movie, starring John Travolta.

Although the circumstances surrounding Christian's casting were tragic (he was brought in to replace River Phoenix, who, just one month before filming was scheduled to begin, collapsed and died of a drug overdose), according to author Rice he was 'utterly convincing as the interviewer, and he made the story all the more powerful by his entirely understandable reactions to the tale. For me, he was plenty young enough to be Daniel Malloy. Christian is in the film so briefly that I can truly say my favourite moments with him are all of his moments.'

Although now familiar to many, the story of River Phoenix's decline is still as fascinating as the night it happened and is as important to Christian's story as it was to Phoenix's own. After all, Phoenix's death provided Christian with a role that would be a highlight of his career.

In little more than twelve years, River Phoenix had established himself as one of the most significant actors of his generation and the least likely to hit the A-list of premature departures. In fact, his unique upbringing by unconventional parents did everything to suggest the opposite. Time and again, his often bold decisions to speak out about the dangers of hard drugs and of his attitudes towards them did nothing but affirm his general aversion to recreational drugs of any sort. His attitude won him the respect and admiration of fans around the world as he was propelled from teen star to cultural icon.

All the same, Phoenix spent as little time as he could in Hollywood. As much as his friends Keanu Reeves and Winona Ryder did their best to retreat from the hype of Tinseltown, so too did Phoenix, deploring what he called Hollywood's 'bad influences and superficial values'. Indeed, other fans, and the Hollywood insiders themselves, have since struggled to make sense of the actor's death. Even a casual observer of tabloid headlines wouldn't have had Phoenix pegged as one likely to run into trouble. It simply beggared belief that the child of hippie parents – someone with such Utopian ideals, who refused meat, dairy and fish products, campaigned for environmental issues such as saving the rainforests and the humane treatment of animals, refused to wear leather and characteristically chose to hide away from the celebrity spotlight – could have died of a drug overdose. It just wasn't possible.

Phoenix's last night on Earth started earlier that Saturday at his suite in the Nikko Hotel, west of Los Angeles. Even room service noted the chaos, including loud music and a highly intoxicated-looking Phoenix, whose demeanour could probably be attributed to drugs and alcohol.

Phoenix wasn't concerned, though, and neither apparently was his party, consisting of Samantha Mathis, his girlfriend at the time and co-star of his latest movie, *The Thing Called Love*; his brother, Leaf; his sister, Rain; and Red Hot Chilli

Peppers bassist Flea. As he made his way across town slumped in the back of his car, however, Phoenix must have wondered how on earth he was going to make it through the evening.

It hit him almost as he arrived at the Viper Room. One waitress noted that, barely able to stand, Phoenix 'kept leaping up and bumping into things. His words were so slurred you could barely understand him.' But still the drinks kept coming.

Although exactly what happened next is unclear, Phoenix moved into a back room behind the corner stage to consume a 'speedball', an often-lethal cocktail of drugs. Phoenix then returned to his table and, without warning, started vomiting. Some of his party took him to the bathroom to clean him up, splashing cold water on his face in their attempts to stop him trembling, but to no avail. By the time they returned to their table, it was clear that the actor was well on the way to becoming an overdose victim.

'He just looked completely stoned,' observed one guest that evening. 'It was quite apparent that he was on something. He was table-hopping and bumping into tables.' Not only that but he was having seizures, falling down hard on the table and sliding away beneath it. Even more frightening was the trouble he was having breathing. Even as he passed Johnny Depp, playing on stage, on his way outside to grab some fresh air with Samantha, Leaf and Rain, his condition was no better. In fact, he was now only minutes away from losing his life. He eventually collapsed on the pavement outside the Viper Room in a fit of violent twitching and thrashing. According to one photographer outside the club, he looked 'like a fish out of water, flapping around the sidewalk like a guppy'. The strange thing, he continues, was that 'people walked by. No crowd formed and no one stopped to help.' It was, after all, Halloween, a night when every oddball in the area was on parade dressed either as a victim of a drive-by shooting or as a bloody surfer cut in two by a surfboard.

As River collapsed, Leaf panicked, rushed into the Viper Room foyer, picked up the phone and dialled 911, begging the emergency services to hurry. The same message was later played repeatedly on radio and television news reports in the aftermath of the tragedy. 'My brother's having seizures,' Leaf sobbed on the tape. 'I'm thinking he had Valium or something. You must get here, please, because he's dying.'

Sadly, it was too late. By the time the medics arrived, just minutes later, River Phoenix was pronounced to be in full cardiac arrest. It was nine minutes before two o'clock on Halloween morning, just three hours after he had arrived at Johnny Depp's club.

'There hasn't been anything this catastrophic and dramatic,' declared *Variety* columnist Amy Archerd, 'since James Dean and Natalie Wood died.' It was a view endorsed in the tributes that swiftly accumulated outside the Viper Room. THE ETERNAL RIVER FLOWS read an inscription on a watercolour etching at the pavement altar festooned with incense candles, while one note lamented A TRUE INDIVIDUAL, WHO WILL BE REMEMBERED, as a teenager stared quietly while others wept. 'It's too sad,' sobbed a man from Glasgow standing next to four girls in baseball caps. 'He was no age at all, was he?' Another visitor to River's shrine noted, 'He had this ability to observe everything going on around him without really being a part of it. He seemed able to separate himself from his surroundings.'

Not everyone was sympathetic, however, and right-wing television and radio chat-show host Rush Limbaugh certainly wasn't, even condemning the media's attention to it. 'From the moment his death was discovered, you would have thought the President of the United States had been assassinated here ... that we've lost some great contributor to the social and human condition,' she railed. 'This guy. Look at his name! River Phoenix! He's the son of a couple of whacked-out hippies.'

Johnny Depp was astounded at this reaction, and a lot other people – among them, probably, Christian – shared his indignation. 'I didn't know him well,' confessed Christian, 'but it all helped to remind me that my own life could have gone that way and that my current lifestyle is working. I just remember thinking [at the time], Does anyone do drugs like that any more? I used to subscribe to that James Dean school of thought. Now I'm just concerned with living as long as I can. As you get older, you get some balance in your life. These days, I'm as clean as I can be.'

For Christian, however, being drafted in to replace Phoenix at the last minute for *Interview with the Vampire* for one week in November 1993 was 'really uncomfortable'. He'd met director Neil Jordan six months before shooting started, 'because I was interested in another role, that of Armand, which was eventually taken by Antonio Banderas. But I really hated Jordan, to be honest with you, because he spent most of the interview on the phone. I was offended by that. I've since found out that he's very shy and has a difficult time communicating. When I heard that they wanted me for River Phoenix's role, I wanted no part of it. Then my agent suggested I donate the money to his charities and ones that I'm involved with.'

Although Christian's was only a supporting role, it was still a highly visible one in a film that grossed a more-than-respectable $105.3 million at the box office. In his review, Roger Ebert opined that the movie's success wasn't surprising, judging that, 'on a scene-by-scene basis, *Interview with the Vampire* is a skilful exercise in macabre imagination'.

Remaining faithful to the detailed vision that has informed all of Anne Rice's novels, and that owes much to a greater taste for realism exhibited by lovers of modern horror fiction, *Interview with the Vampire* was a film about what it might really be like to be one of the undead. The tone of the movie is set by the title, and in the opening scenes, set in San Francisco, the 200-year-old vampire Louis de Pointe du Lac (Brad Pitt) submits to an interview by Christian's journalist Daniel Malloy, just as any serial killer or terrorist bomber might sit down to talk to *60 Minutes*. Du Lac's story begins in the late eighteenth century, in New Orleans, that peculiar city where even today all things seem possible and where, after losing his wife and daughter, Pitt's character threw himself into a life of grief and debauchery. His path crossed that of the vampire Lestat (Tom Cruise), who transformed him into one of his own, and ever since he has wandered the world's great cities, feeding on the blood of his victims.

The initial meeting between Louis and Lestat takes the form of a seduction; the vampire seems to be courting the

younger man, and there is a strong element of homo-
eroticism in the way in which the neck is bared and the
blood pulses. Parallels between vampirism and sex, both gay
and straight, are always there in all of Rice's novels. With
vampirism, of course, the good news is that you can indulge
your lusts night after night, but the bad news is that, if you
stop, you die.

Tom Cruise, who initially seemed to many people an
unlikely choice to play Lestat, is never less than convincing,
and his slight British accent, combined with make-up that is
dramatic without being obtrusive, disguises the clean-cut star
and makes him seem unwholesome in an odd, insinuating
way. Brad Pitt, whose role is probably larger, and who has
been at home as the depraved outlander in films like
Kalifornia, here seems more like an innocent, a young man
who makes unwise choices and lives to regret them.

One of the creepier aspects of the story is the creation of
the child vampire, Claudia, played by Kirsten Dunst, who is
twelve years old when the story takes place. The character
was six in the novel, but even twice as old she is disturbing,
trapped in her child's body as she ages, decade after decade.
Dunst, perhaps with the help of Stan Winston's subtle make-
up, is somehow able to convey the notion of great age inside
apparent youth.

The movie's unique glory is in its look, created by
cinematographer Philippe Rousselot and production
designer Dante Ferretti, whose credits include Scorsese's *The
Age of Innocence* and Gilliam's *The Adventures of Baron
Munchausen*. In *Interview with the Vampire*, Ferretti combines
the elegance of the former and the fantastic images of the

latter to create a vampire world of eerie beauty. The action in the movie largely takes place at night, of course, in old Southern plantations and French Quarter dives, along gloomy back streets and in decadent bordellos. The film truly takes flight when du Lac crosses the ocean on a transatlantic sailing ship and explores the catacombs of Paris. There are scenes set in a vast underground columbarium that's one of the great sets of movie history, where the vampires sleep on shelves reaching up into the gloom.

While in Paris, Louis meets the vampires Armand (Antonio Banderas) and Santiago (Stephen Rea) and begins to understand that he is a member of an international clandestine society. Vampires, of course, need regular supplies of fresh blood, and the details involving its procurement are dismaying to the creatures, who, to live, must constantly feed off the lives of others. Their sadness is manifest in the screenplay and moody direction of (respectively) Anne Rice and Neil Jordan, who both take this subject, with its abundant possibilities for looking ridiculous, and play it as tragedy.

The book's author described the art direction, costumes, lighting, cinematography and craft of the film as 'sumptuous' and 'thrillingly successful' and, whether you loved it or hated it, there was no denying that *Interview with the Vampire* was a breathtaking achievement for everyone concerned, including Christian Slater.

Chapter 8

To Kill A Mockingbird

It was soon after completing his one-week schedule on *Interview with the Vampire* that Christian would take over the role of James Stamphill from Charlie Sheen in Marc Rocco's *Murder in the First*. Based on a powerful true story, the film follows the uplifting and extraordinary relationship between two young men, an Alcatraz convict (Kevin Bacon) and a principled young attorney (Christian), who change each other's life as they change history.

An emotionally rich tale, *Murder in the First* charts one man's descent into inhumanity and another man's determination to retrieve him and reveal the unspeakable brutality of his imprisonment. The unlikely friendship that forms between the idealistic and privileged lawyer and the troubled, deeply withdrawn convict leads to a dramatic struggle marking the beginning of the end of Alcatraz as a penal institution.

According to the movie's production notes, it was in March 1938, in Alcatraz prison, the rocky island institution rising up from the depths of San Francisco Bay, that a man was thrown into a 5ft-high underground vault, naked and alone. A metal door clangs shut and the 6ft-by-9ft room plunges into total darkness. There is total silence. Seawater seeps down the cold stone walls. Mould grows everywhere. There is no window, no bed, no heat, no toilet, no sink, no air and no light.

The man peers into the cold darkness. He is filthy, hungry, struggling to keep his senses alive. The only contact with the outside world comes every few days when food is shoved through a slat in the bottom of the cell door. There is a sound – maybe a voice – and brief sliver of light, and then the hatch is slammed shut. Darkness returns.

The man begins to lose count of the days as they pass. The silence and the blackness blur the passage of time as weeks go by. Months. Years. Then, in June 1941, he finally emerges, dazed, terrorised and incoherent, from the dungeons of Alcatraz. He learns he has spent more than three years in the blackness below. Within hours, in the sunlit prison mess hall, he sees the man he believes responsible for his ordeal and murders him in front of 200 witnesses.

With that single act of vengeance comes the only freedom prisoner Henri Young believes he will have. He is transferred from Alcatraz to the San Francisco city jail, facing a charge of murder in the first degree. As the sun sets on his first day in light in more than three years, Henri Young's long ordeal is changed. Unbeknownst to him, a search for justice in his name is about to begin.

It was, wrote film critic Roger Ebert in his review, the story of Young that made the story, the prisoner who was originally 'arrested for stealing $5 to feed his starving little sister, was later kept in solitary confinement for three years, went berserk, killed a guard, and is now being tried for murder. Stamphill says the system, not the prisoner, is guilty. As the movie opens, Young has been driven into a tiny corner of his mind by the brutal experience of solitary confinement and peers out suspiciously at the world. It is Stamphill's task to win his trust.'

On a more critical note, Ebert continued, 'Most of the film is given over to the relationship between the accused and his lawyer, and Bacon and Slater spend a lot of time in two-shots together, holding intensity contests. Slater, who in certain shots looks curiously like Kevin Costner, is an actor with talent, but he is too young for this role and not confident enough to dial down a little. Hollywood sometimes goes on youth kicks like this, casting kids in their mid-twenties in roles where a substantial character actor is called for. Eventually we stop believing in the story, and then we stop caring.'

Rolling Stone magazine's reviewer, however, didn't entirely agree, stating, 'It's impossible to leave *Murder in the First* without being moved. Bacon dropped 25lb and wore disfiguring make-up to capture Henri's scarred look, but his achievement in the role comes in letting us see the emotional scars left by Henri's ordeal. More than likely you will forgive the compromises; the story of Henri Young needed to be told.'

If we are to believe Ebert in his assertion that perhaps

Christian and Bacon weren't up to the job, it seemed that Gary Oldman was. In his book *Hollywood: The New Generation*, James Cameron Wilson wrote, 'Oldman as a depraved warden stole every scene he was in.'

For Oldman, in his second film with Christian, playing the villain of the piece wasn't that difficult. 'I didn't have to work for it, in part, because it's all there on the page. He was power and, when you have true power, you don't have to shout or get hysterical; people do what you say. Its real control over people. Warden Glenn's just doing his job. He puts on his suit and tie, takes his lunchbox, says goodbye to his two kids and wife, comes into the prison and his whole personality changes. He has authority and he plays a role. And as part of that role, he beat the daylights out of Henri Young.'

The idea of making the film was the brainchild of David L Wolper, whose Wolper Organisation had been developing *Murder in the First* for almost seven years, recalls screenwriter Dan Gordon. When Gordon was first approached with the idea for the story, he jumped at the chance to become involved. 'A true story always interests me,' he reflects. 'This one was special because it had a meaning and a real effect in the closing of Alcatraz. Above all of that, though, it was a fascinating story about the relationship between two young people, which is becoming harder to find.'

Director Marc Rocco, too, was immediately drawn to the story of Henri Young after reading an early version of the script, a fictional drama that Gordon, interestingly enough, had based simply on a handful of newspaper articles he'd read about the case. Rocco then spent another nine months looking deeper into the case, going through record archives, libraries and newspapers, as well as watching literally hundreds of hours of all the newsreel and archival footage he could lay his hands on. 'I didn't want to make this a Hollywood version of a courtroom or prison drama,' he affirms. 'I wanted to play for realism, to try to be accurate to the time and place. I believe that, if you do the research and make as many details as real as possible, you can transcend the time period and make [any film] almost timeless in its own way.'

On top of the archival research he took on, Rocco also made more than fifteen trips to Alcatraz in order to get a feel for the place, conducted interviews with former convicts, guards and attorneys, and even spent an entire weekend locked up alone in solitary confinement at the prison. Even so, it was no easy feat for him to gather all the documentary material together to make it into a film because many of the original court records concerning the case had been destroyed. In fact, they had probably all been shredded when Young's case prompted a federal investigation into punishment practices and the treatment of prisoners at Alcatraz, angering and embarrassing many officials who had proudly pointed to the prison as a model penal institution.

Rocco brought the same commitment to realism and dedication to casting as he did to researching the story. He wanted leading actors who could carry the essentially two-character story and handle highly dramatic monologues. To meet these demands, he first approached Christian.

'Marc and I were friends several years prior to making the film and have always wanted to do something together,' Christian recalls. 'When I read the script for this, I was very excited. I wanted to do it. The story was heartfelt, passionate and dramatic, similar to *To Kill a Mockingbird* or *Inherit the Wind*. The fact that it was based on a true story made it even more interesting and fascinating. It's quite frightening, as well, to think that these events actually took place.'

Rocco admits that the role was something of a departure for Christian. 'Audiences are going to see a Christian Slater they haven't seen before. He is a very good actor and he brought so much to this role that I ended up being able to do much more with the story than I had envisioned.'

Christian's character, James Stamphill, is a fictionalised composite of the attorneys who defended Young. To prepare for his role as the young litigator, Christian attended classes at law school and researched the case. 'James is very naïve in this world of corruption and powerful individuals who manipulate the media,' he observes. 'During the course of the film, his eyes are opened up to doing what's right and defending the innocent man. One thing I admired about the character is that, with all the pressures working against him, he chooses to do the right thing: to do as much as possible to save Henri Young.'

Kevin Bacon's preparation for his role as Henri Young was equally gruelling. 'He spent much of his life since he was seventeen in prison,' explained Bacon. 'When we meet him in the film, he's about to spend three years of his life in solitary confinement. That experience is at the core of the man; it's the essence of who he is and will define him for the rest of his life. Even when out of Alcatraz, in some ways he's still trapped inside that cell, with all the memories of physical and emotional pain.'

Like Marc Rocco, Bacon also spent a night in solitary at

Alcatraz prior to filming in order to gain a greater understanding of Henri's ordeal. He transformed himself not only emotionally and psychologically but also underwent a physical metamorphosis as well, losing more than 25lb in order to resemble the emaciated prisoner's physique, adhering to a strict diet and daily aerobic exercise. He also endured up to an hour and a half in the make-up chair in order to adorn the subtle changes to his character's hair and make-up that mark the progression of years. 'If I have to spend ten minutes in a make-up chair, it's too long,' admitted Bacon, 'but in this film I had a bunch of different looks as you see the character over the course of three years. The effects and images were really very good and strong and helped me get into Henri's mind.'

The *San Francisco Examiner*'s movie critic, Scott Rosenberg, noted as much in his review. 'Bacon's performance is hard-working, respectable; the actor's face is adorned with scars and his frame is emaciated to reflect the rigors of solitary.' But Rosenberg wasn't particularly smitten with Christian in the film, branding him 'a natural wiseguy' and judging him 'a little miscast as the crusading lawyer. This actor has worked a cynical persona for too long to make the transition to idealism comfortably. *Murder in the First* isn't content to document the horrors Henri Young endured; it keeps trumpeting its own significance in scenes of courtroom grandstanding and contrivedly intimate monologues.'

All the same, the general consensus was that *Murder in the First* was a good film, despite some elementary faults here and there. Despite the odd criticisms, Marc Rocco still believes, 'We did a good job. There isn't anything that happens in the movie that wasn't something that happened at Alcatraz.'

Actually, there was one change: the addition of Mary McCasslin, who in the film loves Christian and wants to protect him from ruining his career by taking on the controversial case. It was the only principal part that was created wholly by the writers, but it was also the most difficult role to cast. After screen-testing more than 500 women, the film-makers ended up choosing Embeth Davidtz. 'The movie isn't a love story,' Rocco affirms, 'yet you have to believe her and Christian's relationship. When Embeth came in, she has the strength and maturity and was frankly the only one I believed could play the role. She certainly understood the balance that was needed between being a romantic interest and mentor for Christian's character. They have more of an intellectual connection and friendship. She's more experienced than James and she guides and leads him.'

For Davidtz, the role gave her a unique opportunity to portray a female attorney at a time when women presiding in the courtroom were rare. 'In the 1940s there were only six women attorneys in the state of California,' she says. 'Mary's a woman in a man's business with very little opportunity. She was an exception to the rule, and that appealed to me. This is a film about having the choice in front of you to either serve humanity or yourself, and that is the essence of James's dilemma. It is much more than a courtroom or prison drama because there's such a moral behind it.'

Davidtz was equally enthusiastic about Christian's acting, raving, 'He's doing the part really well.' Indeed, perhaps both enjoyed their parts being compared to many of those played by Spencer Tracy and Katharine Hepburn. 'The film actually does remind me of the Hepburn–Tracy movies,' she admitted to *Premiere* magazine in April 1994, 'except there's less romance.'

However, filming at Alcatraz wasn't quite as straightforward as perhaps was first anticipated. The logistics of filming on an island presented their own set of challenges. For a start, all of the production equipment – trucks, generators and lighting equipment – had to be brought over by boat or barge and offloaded by a crane on to the island, while food and water was transported with the cast and crew on the barge from the mainland each day. And replacing traditional trailer and motorhome dressing rooms was the former Alcatraz hospital ward.

Another problem was the island's 4,000 daily visitors. Filming period drama around tour times in the main cell block, exercise yards and other areas of the prison was certainly made more difficult every time the tour boats arrived in the dock area, and of course the hordes of onlookers who wanted to catch a glimpse of Christian and Kevin only made matters worse. Certainly, the number of tourists more than doubled when word got out that both actors were filming on the island. Now, instead of having people asking, 'Which one is the Birdman's cell?' the punters were walking around asking, 'Where's Christian and Kevin?'

No sooner was Christian's work on *Murder in the First* complete than he started work on yet another movie, which, although filming began in 1994, would not be released until over two years later, in 1996. Leaving Alcatraz and San Francisco and joining Mary Stuart Masterson, he headed back home to New York to film *Bed of Roses*, Michael Goldenberg's romantic drama about a young career girl who is swept off her feet by a shy florist.

The year, however, ended on a sour note when, two nights before Christmas, Christian ran into his third law-breaking problem, this time with the authorities at New York's JFK Airport. He had attempted to board a 6.30pm flight to Los Angeles, neglecting to tell baggage control about the 6.5mm Beretta handgun and the six rounds of ammunition he'd stashed in his black nylon holdall. Matters were made worse when it was discovered that the gun was unregistered and Christian didn't have the federal permit required to transport it from state to state.

After two hours spent in a holding cell and a night at Queens Criminal Court, Christian pleaded guilty to the misdemeanour of attempted weapon possession. He was given three days' community service and sent on his merry way. His light sentence was really a stroke of luck considering he was still serving out his five-year probation for the drink-driving offence from December 1989, violation of which carried a risk of a seven-year sentence.

As if that wasn't enough, he wasn't quite prepared for the legal fracas he would have to face the following April, after *Bed of Roses* was in the can, this time with his former fiancée, Nina Huang, who had filed a palimony lawsuit against Christian in a Los Angeles court. Huang contended that, while the couple had lived together on and off for almost five years, until April 1994, she had abandoned full-time employment and put her own professional goals on hold to work for him. On top of that, she claimed, Christian had vowed to give her half of what he earned during the five years they were together. In the end, Christian paid a settlement, the terms of which have never been publicly released, although Christian's mother's comments at the time give a broad impression. Mary Jo admitted that she was simply pleased to see them go their separate ways, and in the throes of the court case, concerned about Huang's ability to take advantage, she said angrily that Christian 'gave her anything she wanted, but nothing was enough'.

But perhaps Christian wasn't entirely blameless. According to *People Weekly*, he found it hard not to fall in love with the women he had worked with. 'They were beautiful and intelligent,' Christian told Gail Buchalter of the *San Francisco Chronicle*. 'Each embodied everything I have ever desired in a woman. It's almost impossible to avoid feelings of closeness, especially when you're on location. Sometimes it lasts longer than the movie, if not romantically then as a friend.'

Huang, though, was apparently less philosophical. In 1994, when the couple briefly split and Christian took up with model Christy Turlington, she reportedly pressed Christian to sell his Manhattan duplex, the scene of the Turlington trysts, which he did. According to one of those ubiquitous 'friends' who always seem on hand to comment upon showbiz affairs of the heart, his actions revealed that 'they were trying to get over his past affairs'.

If that was the case, it didn't work. The memories lingered on and, on the day of their break-up, the couple were perusing a magazine featuring pictures of several of

Christian's ex-loves. Huang got mad and headed to Hollywood's Chateau Marmont Hotel, where many celebrities notoriously begin and end their relationships (Johnny Depp and Winona Ryder started their overhyped and turbulent relationship, in the same room that John Belushi had killed himself, and years later it was where Olivier Martinez bedded Kylie Minogue). Six days after staying at the famous hotel, running up a bill of $1,864 (charged, of course, to Christian), Huang slapped him with the lawsuit. She was seeking $100,000 plus cash and possessions worth about $2 million in compensation for giving up her screenwriting career to perform such services as 'preparing meals and cleaning residencies'.

If either party was inconsolable after their break-up, then they didn't let it show. Christian had first met the eclectically ethnic Huang through friends in 1990. Three years later, they were living together, and two years after that, they were engaged. Certainly, as a crew member on the set of *Murder in the First* noted, they seemed to have 'a real comfortable relationship. It was kind of weird, watching them walk around Alcatraz, holding hands.'

To her credit, though, Huang didn't mind the dismal setting. On one especially gruelling night on the Rock, says actress Betsy Moore, 'she stayed waiting when we were shooting until 2am. You'd think she'd be home, but she was there for him.'

Others closer to the couple agreed that it looked like Christian was finally ready to get serious and commit. But was he? Even though he didn't set a date for the wedding, he did tell *People* magazine in 1993 that he was feeling kind of settled. 'Even if it gets topsy-turvy,' he noted then, 'we love each other, and we'll see where it goes, but the relationship thing is tricky.'

After this unhappy ending to his first publicly serious relationship, Christian wasn't in any particular hurry to let anyone else into his life, and it would be late 1996 before he became involved with someone new. This time his romantic interest was actress Christina Applegate, whom he had apparently dated before she had hooked up with Johnathon Schaech, going on to marry him almost five years later.

But there was also a time when Christian wasn't really interested in relationships. 'I was always the type of guy who was totally at a loss without a girlfriend, but I really don't have the desire right now,' he vowed in 1997. 'I'm just having a good time, and I think it would take someone really special for me to want to look into having a relationship. Sure, I want to have kids and a wife. I know that. I also know that I'm not ready for it now.'

He found it much easier just to go out with friends. 'I don't have a lot of friends,' he confessed, 'and I don't really want a lot of friends. I need two friends. I trust them; I know they have my best interests at heart. I know they really care about me and I feel fortunate that I've managed to get that in my life. The more friends you have, the more problems you're letting into your life.' And the one thing that Christian didn't need right then was problems.

Part of the process that Christian – like many people – used to distance himself from the problems in his life was to return to work. By early 1994, he had found the solution: he set about producing his first feature-length independent film, titled *Basil*, which, according to *People Weekly*, had started shooting that March. *Basil* was a love story set in London in the 1880s in which Christian played an aristocrat and mentor to a young man in love, played by Jared Leto. Coincidentally, at the time Leto was best known for his role in *My So-Called Life* and would later go on to play Winona Ryder's boyfriend in her self-exec-produced *Girl, Interrupted* – a movie, incidentally, that won Angelina Jolie an Oscar, which according to some put Ryder's nose out of joint.

As online film critic Christopher Null noted, *Basil* was 'a pleasant costume drama yet terribly predictable and featured Jared Leto and Christian Slater in the most unlikeliest [*sic*] of roles as the two British subjects of yesteryear. The tale that unfolds is simplistic and easy to second-guess, but at least it's watchable. Slater surprises with the best performance in the group, but ultimately that doesn't redeem the film for being a terribly tepid tale that doesn't have much to say.'

Chapter 9

Hard Time

Christian's last mainstream movie, *Bed of Roses*, was regarded in many quarters as being something of an odd movie – especially for Christian, who film critic Roger Ebert considered was far better as 'a cool, laconic outsider than as a dreamer with a song in his heart'. Ebert was unconvinced by Christian's performance in the movie, simply because 'the story lays it on so thick, he was simply buried by the material'.

In this, Ebert is probably right, but Christian might also have suspected that the biggest downfall about the film was him. As bad as the critical reception was, *Bed of Roses* stumbled even harder when it met its first audience. It opened in January 1996, just one month ahead of Christian's first action flick, and most agreed with Ebert that the film, although billed as a romantic comedy, generally had 'nothing funny about it'. And, like Ebert, most thought that Christian so often plays a smart-alec that it's confusing to see him playing a straight-shooting, vulnerable man who doesn't want to blow his chance at love. As the *San Francisco Examiner's* movie critic, Barbara Shulgasser, correctly noted, 'You keep expecting him to say, "Just kidding. I don't really love you."'

One can't help but wonder why there was so much critical objection to Christian's performance. When one considers that in the modern fairy tale *Untamed Heart* he played a strange, enchanted orphan boy who maybe, just possibly, had the heart of a baboon beating inside his chest, a role for which he was fawned over, it's difficult to see why people then took such exception to his part in *Bed of Roses*. He was, after all, playing a similarly poetic role. Perhaps the problem was that both audiences and critics weren't sure whether they were supposed to view the movie as a romantic fable.

The story revolves around a man named Lewis Farrell (Christian), a former stock trader with a heart of pure gold who gave up the rat race after the death of his wife and child and now operates an obscure little florist shop in New York so that he can watch the joyous expressions on the faces of his customers when he delivers flowers to them. But that's not all: he also has the peculiar habit of sitting in with the grade-schoolers for story hour at the local public library and sending lavish floral arrangements to perfect strangers.

Written by first-time writer and director Michael Goldenberg, the film begins with just such a delivery. While walking the streets one night, Lewis looks up into the window of an apartment building just in time to catch Lisa (Mary Stuart Masterson) at her lowest ebb, sobbing into the curtains after a particularly intense day during which, at the very moment she landed her biggest professional deal, she was informed that her foster father had passed away. And, if that wasn't enough, her pet goldfish had also died.

For some reason, Lewis decides to follow her to work, find out her name and address, and send her a glorious bouquet of flowers, without a card. Instead of being cheered up by the gift, though, Lisa is nearly driven insane through not knowing who sent them. After all, she isn't the romantic type, and she doesn't want romance from her men, either; a hard-working investment banker, Lisa has no time for affairs of the heart. As her wisecracking best friend, Kim (Pamela Segall), puts it, men are 'night lights' for her – a way of easing the loneliness of her evenings.

When Lisa finally discovers that it was Lewis who sent the arrangement, she freaks out, first because some weirdo stranger has been following her, and second because he offers to open up a whole world outside her safe cocoon of work. From the moment they first meet, Lewis decides that Lisa is the one. He's ready for all of it – intimacy, commitment, romance, family – but she can't deal with any of it.

As many critics noted, *Bed of Roses* was really Mary Stuart Masterson's film. Since starring in 1991's *Fried Green Tomatoes* and Johnny Depp's *Benny and Joon* two years later, by the time she landed the role of Lisa her features had become sharper and more striking. She's a formidable presence on screen, but she also has an engagingly neurotic comedy style. 'Do you often go to, uh, story hour?' she asks Lewis after a visit to the library, and, as the *Washington Post*'s movie critic, Hal Hinson, noted, watching her advance and retreat –

sometimes in the same moment – as she works through her conflicting impulses is the movie's greatest pleasure.

The problem, though, even to Hinson, was that 'Lisa comes across as a real person and Lewis does not. As a character, Lisa may be a cliché, the modern career woman who hides in her work, but Masterson gives her some grit and psychological shading. Lewis, on the other hand, appears to be some sort of green-thumbed Peter Pan, with a rooftop meadow that serves as an inner-city Elysian fields for the couple's budding affair.' Hinson continued that, as Goldenberg presents him, 'Lewis is the handsome prince who kisses the cheek of the slumbering princess and teaches her how to love.

'But Slater, with his downcast eyes and monotone drawl, makes the character appear soupy and immature. Lisa, despite her troubles, doesn't seem to need a fairy-tale prince to bring her to life. Goldenberg keeps telling us how great this guy is, how perfect, but, compared to Lisa, Lewis seems scrawny, lost in the clouds. In the real world, you feel Lisa would tuck in his shirt tail, pat his little bottom and send him on his way.'

So that was *Bed of Roses*, a movie that – as another critic complained – starts to come apart very quickly. 'The last hour presents a series of concocted crises, some more interesting than others, all of them manufactured to stretch the film to feature length.'

If the unfavourable reviews of *Bed of Roses* left Christian feeling troubled, he didn't have long to mourn. One month later, his next movie was playing across more than 2,000 screens in America to rave reviews, taking in over $70

million in its first two weeks of release and sitting at the top
of the of US box-office listings before being dethroned by
Jackie Chan's *Rumble in the Bronx*.

Broken Arrow was Hong Kong cult favourite director John
Woo's second American directional feature, offering him a
bigger budget ($60 million), bigger stars and bigger special
effects than his first Hollywood outing three years earlier. If
nothing else, the film demonstrated Woo's extraordinary
capability of staging noisy fight scenes and spectacular
explosions, but for some the picture was nowhere close to
the league of Andy Davis's *The Fugitive* or Tony Scott's *Top
Gun* when it came to crafting smart action with intriguing
characters and dialogue.

As *New York Times* writer Janet Maslin put it, however,
Broken Arrow packed an impressive wallop and certainly held
some trump cards. 'Killer special effects, John Travolta as an
irresistible bad guy, Duane Eddy sometimes twanging his
baritone guitar on the soundtrack and casual threats about
nuclear destruction of the American Southwest made for an
over-the-top action blow-out that marks a big step forward
for its director, who has long since earned a cult following
after directing Jean-Claude Van Damme in the much more
gruesome 1993 movie *Hard Target*. Woo orchestrates his
giddy, daring stunts on a newly spectacular level. Things crash
or explode here at regular intervals, with virtually non-stop
acrobatics in between. The screenplay – by Graham Yost,
who also penned *Speed* – seldom wastes time on anything
but the taunts required to get from one fight to the next.'

Woo later confessed that he found the filming of *Broken
Arrow* a trying process and an unpleasant experience. 'The

studio executive tried to block any changes to the script, some of the people we had to work with were not good and the line producer would control and change things behind my back. Luckily the chairman of Fox let me make some of the final decisions, but all the game-playing really comes out in the final product: the style is incomplete.'

'*Hard Target* was my first movie in Hollywood and I never knew there were so many problems to making films in Hollywood. A lot of things were so frustrating, like the politics, the games, the meetings and everything. It was quite an experience. After *Hard Target*, I stopped making movies for almost two years and tried to find the right material, tried to find something really close to my style. But it was hard. Even though there are a lot of great writers in Hollywood and a lot of writers who wanted to work with me, it was still hard to find the right things that would fit my style.

'I took a lesson from *Hard Target*, and so when it came to *Broken Arrow* I didn't want to let it happen again. So that's why, in *Broken Arrow*, I adopted a Hitchcock thriller style. I got inspiration from Hitchcock's *North by Northwest*. I tried to make this movie all in one tone and kept the excitement from the beginning till the end. I tried to make everything even, especially the action. I still kept a little style while keeping the excitement of the action. And the violence – you feel the violence, but it's not exaggerated. And there's charming characters: there's charm and humour, and it seemed to end just right.'

Maybe this is true, but, as many viewers observed, the film was marred by a number of continuity errors in the film. The only excuse that could be offered for such careless blunders was that, supposedly, the film was running over budget, and so Woo couldn't reshoot any footage. Another problem, however, was the fact that the film had three different editors, each of whom had his own ideas about what footage should and shouldn't be used.

Despite such problems, however, the film is still regarded as one that broke new ground in the full-throttle action-adventure field, and perhaps much of that was down to the casting, the pairing of John Travolta with Christian proving a powerful draw to bring the primal power of the *Broken Arrow* premise to the screen.

In addition to appreciating the opportunity to extend their on-screen personas, John and Christian jumped at the chance to work with Woo, a master at blending high-voltage action and character-driven stories. Out of the two, it was Travolta who was offered the choice of which character he wanted to play, and in the end the veteran actor chose the villain of the piece simply because he hadn't played a bad-guy role for some time.

Not that Christian was concerned. All that mattered to him was that he was in a John Woo film. 'I'm a huge fan of John Woo,' he explained at the time. 'I've wanted to work with him since I saw *The Killer* several years ago.'

Although Woo's idea was originally to have Christian's character die at the end of the movie, the studio nixed the idea because of Christian's popularity with teenage girls. Travolta, on the other hand, who had passed on several action-film projects since his comeback in *Pulp Fiction* just two years earlier, and who was now declaring that this would probably be his last action film (although he would return exactly one year later to star in Woo's *Face/Off*), was initially so impressed with Woo's signature visual style that, after being introduced to his work by Quentin Tarantino, and after watching a few of Woo's films for himself, was completely sold on Woo's work in the action genre. 'It had a sense of art to it, which is very unusual. He's a real artist at delivering this kind of film.' Like his co-star, Travolta just wanted to enter Woo's world of visionary celluloid.

Producer Bill Badalato admitted that he shares the same view. 'John Woo is one of the most unique directors with whom I've ever been associated. He has a particular vision and a knack for placing the camera for complicated moves that really pay off.' It's a view that was re-echoed by Christopher Godsick (who, interestingly enough, was partnered with Woo and co-producer Terence Chang at WCG Entertainment), who observed, 'A John Woo film typically has intricately choreographed actions scenes that don't appear choreographed. Equally important, his films have fleshed-out characters who carry a particular code of honour. And *Broken Arrow* is certainly no exception.'

In addition to the casting of Christian and John Travolta, another bonus was bringing in Samantha Mathis to play park ranger Terry Carmichael, who in the film teams up with Christian to combat Travolta and his gang. As Terence Chang put it, 'Samantha brings a kind of sweetness and vulnerability to the character in addition to the toughness. She lets you like this person and care about her.' Mathis, in turn, appreciated Terry's central predicament. 'She gets involved in her worst nightmare,' meaning her own death and the possible destruction of the pristine desert she patrols by nuclear terrorists. 'It's everything she has ever fought against.'

It's a fear shared by Kurtwood Smith's Secretary of Defense (and, probably, the one in real life, too), who murmurs at one point, 'I don't know what's scarier: the fact that there are missing nuclear weapons or that this happens so often that there's actually a term for it.'

This is a reference to the title of the movie, which is actually used in a military context, being a code term for a lost nuclear device. 'There have been several broken arrows,' Christopher Godsick explains. 'For instance, in 1989 a nuclear submarine, with two warheads aboard, sank 300 miles off the coast of Norway and was never recovered by the navy. Also, nuclear missiles were never retrieved from a B-1 bomber that crashed in the Mediterranean. So our story is not as far-fetched as you might think.'

Such real-life incidents provided the inspiration for screenwriter Graham Yost, who came across the unusual term from a source who informed him of yet another broken-arrow situation regarding a bomber and its nuclear cargo that were lost in the Sea of Japan for several years before they could be retrieved. The possibilities of additional recent incidents were also hinted at.

Despite such timely issues being a serious threat and a global concern, Yost's primary goal, of course, was to give audiences an incredible ride. He acknowledged that his *Speed* and *Broken Arrow* scripts reflect his own tastes in entertainment: 'I'd rather just have fun with the genre than be heavy and brutal. I enjoy trying to think of everything that could possibly go wrong for the characters in a given situation and clever ways for them to get out of trouble.'

Certainly, Yost's script was an important selling point for Woo. 'Besides providing a lot of great action sequences, the screenplay has some great characters. I also saw the themes which I've employed in many of my other films: tragic friendship, loyalty, betrayal and honour.'

Adding to the excitement during filming, Slater, Mathis, Travolta and a top crew of stunt people were seemingly placed in danger from a hailstorm of pyrotechnics, bullets, hand grenades, engulfing fireballs and diving helicopters passing inches above their heads, but all under the careful eye of stunt co-ordinators Allan Graf and Gary Hymes.

Christian readily embraced much of the stunt work. In one heart-stopping piece, shot during the third phase of production in the lowlands of central Montana, the script called for his character to fall off a speeding train, get dragged and then pull himself along underneath, all of which he carried off flawlessly. 'We took all the precautions,' remembers Hymes, 'but I'm sure it was pretty scary for Christian to be under the train. The fact that he did the stunt himself added much validity and credibility to the scene. We were fortunate that he and our other actors were athletic and were able to do quite a bit of their own stunts.'

Slater and Travolta's athletic prowess also came in handy for the film's opening boxing sequence, which establishes the different levels of the relationship between the two friends as they trade punches, and former world boxing champion Carlos Palomino was brought in to teach them the basics. In addition, Travolta, Slater and Mathis were individually trained in the handling of various weapons by weapons specialist Robert 'Rock' Galotti, a decorated combat veteran who participated with the US Forces in the Grenada and Desert Storm campaigns. Given John Woo's penchant for unbridled action and gunplay, it isn't surprising that Galotti found *Broken Arrow* to be one of his most challenging projects. A veteran 'armourer' who has worked hard to build a list of accident-free films, including *Forrest Gump, Born on the Fourth of July* and *Hard Target,* Galotti recalls, 'John Woo likes weapons, and he likes gunfire. In *Broken Arrow,* we had about 60,000 rounds of ammunition, and we shot every single round, if not more.'

One of the more light-hearted moments that occurred during shooting happened in Montana. 'John and Christian and I threw a party for the crew,' recalls Mathis. 'We got a karaoke machine and they put on "You're The One That I Want", and the next thing I know John drops to his knees and sings, "I got chills, they're multiplyin'," and I went with it. He picked me up, he spun me around – we did the whole thing. It was the most unbelievable completion of a childhood dream, ever. I thought, Now I can die a happy woman. I've danced with John Travolta.'

When *Detour* magazine caught up with Mathis for a feature in December 1995, she even leaped to her feet to demonstrate the way she poked her finger into Travolta's chest and strutted him across the room while lip-synching the words, 'You better shape up.' Even though she'd seen *Grease* about twenty times in the theatre when she was a child and had been completely blown away with the fact that she had just finished working with the star of that film, she was just as excited about explaining the story of *Broken Arrow* to *Detour*'s Dennis Hensley. 'John and Christian play government pilots, and they're carrying bombs on their B-3 bomber, and John basically ejects Christian out of the plane because he's going to steal the bombs and hold the government ransom. I play a park ranger who finds Christian and together we save the universe. And I got to wear the same outfit for four months. I wanted to burn it afterwards, although it *was* very flattering; it's like khaki by Armani.'

Mathis also related that working with John Woo was lovely, describing him as 'one of the most gentle, soft-spoken directors that I've worked with, which is astounding considering he's known for some of the most violent films … He was very sweet with me, and it was amazing to watch him work, because the way he uses a camera is unlike anything I've ever seen before. He would find a way to shoot a sequence from eight different angles and, when you finally saw that sequence edited together, it was like a ballet. That's what I think is so amazing about his violence. It's not gory violence; it's really quite beautiful. It's elegant. And it's like a dance.'

Samantha was just as enthusiastic about being reunited with Christian. 'We haven't really changed that much. I think we've both grown up a lot, but I didn't find him to be affected by the business in any sort of negative, jaded way.' And the fact that the pair had been romantically involved during the shooting of *Pump Up the Volume* five years earlier didn't bring with it any awkwardness, either. Besides, according to Mathis, it was only 'for a minute, towards the end of filming, after our first kiss in the film'.

Although the film offered Christian the opportunity to acquaint himself with the energetic side of action film-making, and although he said himself that he'd enjoyed playing the character and working with both Woo and Travolta and being reunited with Samantha Mathis for a second time, in the years that followed, the word around Hollywood was that Christian hadn't much enjoyed the experience and, like Travolta, wasn't really interested in making another action flick. Maybe that's why he settled on a much simpler role for his next movie – at least, for the time being.

Julian Po was a startling and offbeat story, told with the placid inevitability of a fairy tale. As film critic Ian Hodder complained, however, going to see the movie was 'akin to doing your laundry in an unknown neighbourhood. It's interesting to watch the locals go about their business, but you forget all about them on the drive home.'

In Britain's *Sight and Sound* magazine, meanwhile, Edward Lawrenson gave a more precise summary of the film in his review. 'Sometime after arriving in the small, deadbeat town where he plans to commit suicide, the eponymous Julian Po (Christian) says he's "pretty used to being anonymous". Despite recording his thoughts on a portable tape recorder (a device which recalls *The King of Marvin Gardens*, 1972, starring an equally introspective Jack Nicholson, an actor whose mannerisms Christian Slater has done a good job of mimicking from *Heathers* onwards), this is about as close as we get to a reason why Po should want to die.

'But it provides an apt comment on the film. With efficient if unremarkable direction by Alan Wade, an unusually restrained, somewhat muffled performance by Slater and a series of undistinguished, characterless locations, an air of workmanlike anonymity hangs over *Julian Po*. There are even parallels between the way Po seems to arrive in the town as if from nowhere – he hails from the city and has never before seen the ocean is all the backstory we get – and the cloudy origins of Wade's debut film, which since it was completed in 1997 has languished for three years without a UK release.

'It's in the curiously bloodless depiction of small-town life that *Julian Po* suffers most. Despite the fact he's long since decided against taking his own life, Po is ultimately driven to suicide by the townsfolk's determination to hold him to his word. It's a downbeat ending and an implicit critique of the conformist pressures bearing down on members of seemingly untroubled, close-knit communities.

'But aside from a few quietly menacing moments (a barber imagines what it would be like to slit Po's throat as he sits waiting to be shaved; Po's creepy hotelier asks him, "Are you a nigger?"), there's little in Wade's communal portrait to suggest any darker undercurrents. It's almost all affectionate, good-hearted stuff. Numbering among its population well-meaning eccentrics (a young wife gives Po a Bible to study; a garage attendant and part-time De Niro impersonator hatches dreams of going to Hollywood; a priest happily announces his loss of faith to his congregation, all turned out in their Sunday best), the town would seem to be an embodiment of the land of good old-fashioned neighbourliness we all thought had disappeared.

'Drifting along agreeably Capra-esque lines for the most part, the film's sudden sour ending doesn't quite wash. Observing a change that's come over him, the now serene Po remarks midway into the film, "There's a kindness here." It's a sign of Wade's scrupulous fence-sitting (a white picket fence, perhaps) that the supreme irony of this comment is only revealed retrospectively, but otherwise there's little to dissuade us from taking it at face value.

'The unbearably fey romantic subplot involving Po and Sarah doesn't help. Having had a vision of Po well before his arrival, the dreamy and father-figure-fixated Sarah declares her love to Po immediately on meeting him; Po responds with a line which even an unreconstructed sentimentalist like Franco Zeffirelli would balk at using: "You're so beautiful. I could go on living forever for you." Later on, in another cringe-inducing aside, Po urges a few of the locals to chase their dreams, because "life's too short". Of course he's right, but eighty-three minutes of this stodgy, airless film is likely to make what time we have on Earth seem just that little bit longer.'

If the production notes are to be taken at face value, however, *Julian Po* is a far, far better film than any review could convey. According to the Cypress Films write-up, the film asks what happens when an ordinary man – a man who considers himself unimportant, perhaps even anonymous – chances upon a cloistered mountain community that hasn't seen a stranger since the Civil War. As the film's protagonist discovers, in such an insular place, even an amusing bookkeeper can become a very important person, simply by being himself. In the film's darkly comic universe, however, the bookkeeper's newfound cachet proves to be something of a mixed blessing.

Thirty-year-old Julian Po has no intentions of changing anyone's life, least of all his own. He's simply taking his first ever vacation, driving to the one place he's always longed to go: the seashore. He has one suitcase and a new hand-held tape recorder, on which he is documenting his life, even though, by his own admission, there's not much to document.

The uneventful landscape of Po's life changes when his car breaks down in the mountains and he treks to a small village whose name has been eroded from the signpost at its outskirts. Arriving in the no-name town, he takes a room at Vern's Boarding House, a building that, according to Vern, is perpetually devoid of guests. Po plans to bathe, sleep and retrieve his car the following day, but when he gets up the next day the car is gone.

Three days pass. There's no train or bus, no apparent way to leave the town. Po eats at the town's only restaurant, takes solitary walks and sits alone in his room. He talks to no one, confiding his thoughts and observations with only his tape recorder.

Despite – or, perhaps, because of – Po's extremely mild-mannered nature, the townspeople are suspicious of him. They track his every movement with increasing paranoia, wary of his reasons for idling in a dull place where he doesn't know a soul. They speculate that he is a drug runner, a murderer, a terrorist, a bomber. Finally, several prominent citizens, including the mayor (Harve Presnell) and the sheriff (Frankie R Faison), corner Po in the town café. Their questioning escalates and Po's answers about his broken-down car and his seaside vacation go unheard. The townspeople are convinced that he has come to kill someone, and finally, in order to placate them, he blurts out that he came there to kill himself.

With this declaration, Julian Po's life changes irrevocably.

Like a prince in a fairy tale, the town seems to wake from a deep slumber. The villagers embrace Po as a liberator, a saviour. They express their deep admiration for his courage and principles. They make offerings of clothing and food, sexual favours and tools with which to effect his suicide. They tell him their troubles, seeing in him a wisdom and clarity that he has never claimed to have. Characters such as Clarence and Potter overhaul their lives after talking to Po, who really is just being polite.

No one believes in Po more than Sarah (played by Robin Tunney, who, like Neve Campbell, first found fame in *The Craft*), a beautiful, melancholy young woman who falls in love with him immediately upon hearing of his impending self-destruction. She tells him that she has been waiting for him all her life – and, indeed, it seems that she has. She passionately embraces him and his destiny.

For the first time ever, Julian Po is happy, love and admired. But how long can this last? Even as fame and power spread, the pressure builds on him to do what he said he came there to do. Events begin to spin out of control and Po finds that his words have gained a terrifying momentum.

Meanwhile, for Christian, life was shortly to imitate art, and his own fame was about to spin out of control.

Chapter 10

Very Bad Things

At 7.30am on 11 August 1997, a month before *Julian Po* was released in America, the LAPD arrived at Jacques Petersen's Wilshire Boulevard complex in downtown Los Angeles in response to a neighbour's complaint. The police were there to clean up what would best be described as the mess from the night before. That night, Christian had stayed at Petersen's apartment in Westwood, Los Angeles, with his girlfriend, fashion editor Michele Jonas, and Petersen, who had brought his own girlfriend, Petra Barrett Brando, Marlon's adopted daughter.

The police reports of the incident describe how, on their arrival, the officers found in the stairwell a half-dressed young man whom they 'immediately recognised as Christian Slater', who was 'swinging his arms and yelling incoherently'. The officers then attempted to subdue him, but he responded by pushing one of them, officer Julio

Flores, against a wall and tried to snatch his gun. After a lengthy struggle, they rendered Christian unconscious with a control hold, but when he came to and found himself in handcuffs he started kicking again, violently, and had to be fully shackled in ankle restraints as well.

Christian was of course put under arrest and charged with three counts of assault with a deadly weapon and a further count of battery. Although Christian initially disputed the charges, he was convicted of sitting on top of Jonas and punching her in the face, and when Petersen tried to pull him off her the two men became embroiled in a fight during which Christian bit his host in the ribcage. After fleeing the apartment, he then assaulted the building's maintenance man before taking refuge in the stairwell. The police were on the premises in minutes.

When Christian recovered consciousness, he told officers Flores and Behnke that he had been drinking for the two days before the assault and taking heroin and cocaine the night before. On top of that, he later admitted that, before leaving Petersen's apartment, he had attempted to kill himself by jumping from the window.

Hollywood, of course, made it easy for Christian. Released on $500,000 bail, he checked into rehab and issued a statement through his lawyer that stated, 'Christian Slater deeply regrets the incident and is taking action to ensure this kind of thing will not happen again.' The statement continued to quote Christian as saying, "'I've been acting since the age of eight, and I have been a celebrity for a long time. And when you're a celebrity, you start believing you can act off the screen any way you want, without consequence.'"

Christian later claimed that the cause of his behaviour was low self-esteem. 'It doesn't matter how famous you are, what kind of car you drive or who you're dating, if your head is telling you that you suck, all you ever want is to escape from that. I'm just dealing with that now.' He went on to profess his sympathy with fellow actor Robert Downey Jr: 'We both suffer from a disease that's like a tornado. It causes wreckage in your life and it tells you that you don't have a problem, so you spend all your time blaming everyone else.'

This time, however, others were blaming Christian, which was perhaps something he hadn't counted on. Matters were also made worse when Christian's girlfriend, Michele Jonas, took out a restraining order, preventing him from approaching her, and officer Julio Flores sued him for 'emotional distress' and 'severe injuries'.

As Britain's *Neon* magazine correctly noted, 'The film industry is a great enabler. There is always an agent, a manager, a publicist, a producer, someone to stand guard in front of the outside world, to clean up the mess and make the excuses – which is odd, given that almost every director [Christian] ever worked with has remarked on his professionalism, his commitment, his grasp of the job at hand. But when the cameras were switched off, for exactly the same reasons, it was only natural for him to do what he thought was expected, what hard-living, hell-raising young movie stars were supposed to do on their day off.'

It seems almost ironic that Christian now sees the night of 10 August 1997 as an 'incredible gift', because everyone knows the facts. 'The cat's out of the bag,' he jokes. 'I'm insane.' Yet, if an everyday Joe Bloggs had behaved in the same manner, it would simply not have been acceptable, or tolerated, no matter how many excuses were offered.

Christian's behaviour that night certainly forced him to look at himself more closely. 'I blanked on the whole thing,' he later admitted. 'I went over to this place, consumed a lot of drugs and alcohol. The fight that happened wasn't between me and the girl at all; it was between me and [myself]. After the fight, I tried to kill myself by jumping off the balcony. They pulled me back in. I made a mad dash for the door. I was trying to get out of there.'

Later, of course, he would become more elaborative in his telling of his attempted suicide. 'I remember going to that apartment, walking out on the balcony on the fourteenth floor and having the thought go through my head,' he recalls. 'It scared me and there was nobody there who I felt comfortable enough to talk with about it. I was already in an uncomfortable place. Then, once I started to imbibe, I acted on it. Not thinking clearly; not thinking at all. Having chemicals affect my brain. I just wanted to end it. This was horrible, my night in hell. I was wiped out, totally. Completely out of my mind.' Then, the day after the incident, Christian continues, 'I knew that I had a problem. Three days later I checked myself into rehab and was incommunicado.'

Looking back, he recognises that he was coming loose at the seams. 'I take full ownership of the incident. I haven't shown any great character, doing drugs and alcohol. But drugs, they're just there, aren't they? I'm not a real big-time druggie; I'm a drinkie. I always start with the drinks. I have the potential to be a guy who'll hang out at a crackhouse, but it's also within me to be a Buddhist. It's "which direction will I go in?" Anything that can affect me from the neck up should be cut out. If I could give up thinking, I'd do that as well. Thinking, unfortunately, is something that I have to contend with.'

He wouldn't have long to mourn, however. Less than two weeks later, according to *Variety*, he was apparently in talks about a possible role in a picture titled *Very Bad Things*, in which, if he accepted the job (which he did), he would star as a bridegroom-to-be whose hellish bachelor party takes a turn for the worse when one of the party guests kills a hired prostitute. At the time, though, it wasn't clear whether the talks were carrying on while Christian was in a recovery clinic, being treated – according to his younger brother – for an undisclosed addiction (more than likely drug and alcohol problems).

If it's true that only in Hollywood can a celebrity's troubles be swiftly spun by the publicity mill into a positive thing, then Christian's troubles hadn't by all accounts been in vain, or even derailed his career – well, not as much as Winona Ryder's career had suffered after she had been caught shoplifting at Saks Fifth Avenue in Beverly Hills; almost one year later, in October 2002, she was sentenced to 480 hours of community service and three years' probation and had to pay thousands of dollars in fines, and it seems that her career has never recovered. For Christian, however, it was an entirely different matter. Even the production company behind *Very Bad Things*, Interscope, were excited. On reading Peter Berg's script and hearing of Christian's wild party antics, the Hollywood bad boy was considered the perfect choice for the role they were now looking to fill.

Berg was equally excited about having Christian in the movie, even though he hadn't had the actor in mind initially. 'I was sitting watching TV late at night and *Heathers* was showing,' he recalls. 'I hadn't seen it in a long time, and there was something there which sparked the idea. [Christian's] ability to blend charm and be sinister is very hard to find, but he's capable of doing both at once as an actor. And dealing with him as a person has never been anything other than a very easy, very pleasurable thing.'

Berg was equally sympathetic about the unfortunate circumstances that had befallen Christian. 'Christian knows, and everyone knows, that the real Christian Slater isn't the kid who got arrested that night in Westwood. He had a rough night, which I'm sure most of us have had at one time or another. He just had a very rough night.'

In his 1997 biography of Winona Ryder, Dave Thompson echoed this sentiment. 'There are times in everybody's life when, suddenly and inexplicably, everything seems to go wrong.'

For Ryder, this disaster occurred when she neared her twentieth birthday, a time when she was closer to that state than she had ever felt before. She kept working, simply because she didn't know what else she could do. Still suffering from insomnia, and still enduring the attention of the gutter press, she admits that she went through much of *Bram Stoker's Dracula* feeling 'tired, tense and not very happy', a state of mind that was only intensified by the knowledge that everyone else on the set expected her to be smiling, confident and strong.

Finally, during a break in the filming schedule, Winona

visited a doctor, whose diagnosis baffled her. 'Anticipatory nostalgia' and 'anticipatory anxiety' were conditions that Winona hadn't even heard of, but the doctor assured her they were quite normal – that is, normal side-effects of an identity crisis.

It's entirely possible that Christian was suffering from the same condition. Four months after his 'wild party antics', for which Christian was sentenced to ninety days in jail, his lawyer, Michael Nasatir, appealed the sentence, asking that Christian's time in rehab be accepted in lieu of incarceration time. His pleas, however, fell on deaf ears. During a ruling held on 9 January 1998, Christian was ordered to report to the Los Angeles County Jail five days later to begin serving his full ninety days. On 14 January, the day after his latest film, *Hard Rain*, premiered in Los Angeles, Christian swapped the luxurious trappings of his home in the Hollywood Hills for a far less glamorous prison cell.

These days, however, Christian paints a much more vivid picture of the sequence of events that led to his imprisonment and what he had done to make things better: 'I was at the premiere for *Hard Rain* and there were all the cameras, questions, lights, the whole thing, but I knew that the very next day I had to go and surrender myself to the authorities. It was phenomenal; it was the two opposite sides to the coin. I thought, Jesus, this is crazy! It was almost as if I'd gone to an island. I've been through times where I felt lost, abandoned and completely lonely. It is then that you discover what you're made of. I used to repeat a line to myself: "Adversity doesn't deal with character; adversity reveals character." Even the night before I surrendered myself, I was getting a new perspective on things. I think that was the point when I started asking myself why and how I'd got so lost, and what I needed to do to not feel that way.

'So I started to make a list of things I hadn't yet accomplished. I asked myself what I had to do and ticked them off as I went through them. Education was the main thing, so I went back to school and got my high-school diploma. I felt great and thought, Yeah, I've done that. The sense of being able to see something all the way through and accomplish it was cool. After that, I started taking acting classes. That was really helpful for me. It gave me confidence.

'I did karate too – I'd never really felt too comfortable with my fighting skills – and I ran the LA marathon: four hours, twenty-six minutes. It was pretty good. If you're a guy who's famous for his exterior, ageing can freak you out. I didn't even think past twenty-four! I've certainly been through periods where I haven't been at peace with my appearance, but I'm comfortable with how things are now. I've started to take care of myself – and there are many more roles to play now I'm older.'

Christian is also proud of himself for not panicking when, on one occasion, a shark swam near him. Some day, he promised, he might even touch one. 'I've tried other things,' he says. 'I tried to get into flying helicopters or planes or riding horses. I've always envied people who have that kind of passion – like John Travolta; he's got that plane thing. No matter what, he can go and be a pilot. Me, I kind of feel like, no matter what, I could become a scuba instructor.'

Christian found it equally simple to explain how he got into trouble in the first place. 'At that time, I was upset. There were some dark days. I was just trying to bury my head in the sand, and I was scared and lost. I really didn't know who I was. You walk around like this empty shell, and people are throwing adulation at you, and you're thinking, I really haven't earned this. I don't get it; I don't know what you want. So you tend to gravitate towards people who are doing the same sorts of things, hanging out with people who are encouraging you to lose yourself. Some of the people I was hanging out with at that time lost themselves to the extent that they are no longer here; they didn't make it.

'Drugs can be a great thing if you want to escape from yourself. I got arrested. I got in trouble. I was just doing well. But in a way, it was an incredible intervention; it was a clear-cut message. I was given a real opportunity [in jail] to take some time, step outside and step away from the career I had.'

As for *Hard Rain*, the movie whose opening preceded Christian's time in jail, the film critic from the *San Francisco Examiner* noted that 'it's fast-moving, it's got fine special effects, the hero and heroine are pure and quick-thinking, the bad people die badly, and the script draws its fair share of laughs and you can walk out of the theatre into the afternoon drool and figure you haven't wasted your ticket money … It's one of those rare movies where you don't mind if people around you shout when the bullets start to fly or talk out loud at the screen. The flick is meant to be talked at, to get people to cheer and jeer and spill their popcorn.

'The story is pretty simple. The town of Huntingburg is caught in non-stop rain and, as the worst of the flood comes on, an armoured truck carrying $3 million breaks down in the rising water. Guards Christian and Ed Asner are confronted by a gang of robbers, led by Morgan Freeman, in an eerie scene lit by spotlights on a pickup truck, the two sides shouting across a flooded road at each other, rain spattering through the headlights.

'The confrontation sets off a chain of events that finds Christian hiding the money under water, then fighting everybody who wants a piece of it while flood waters keep rising and rising, setting up one crazed escape after another. There are some riveting scenes: speedboats crashing through the stained-glass windows of a church, a shootout in a cemetery with crosses sliding under water, bullets skimming off concrete angels and a jet-ski chase through the flooded halls of a school, lights flashing along the walls, wild colours everywhere. It's a marriage of visions from writer Graham Yost, director Mikael Salomon, photographer Peter Menzies Jr and special-effects supervisor John Frazier – a reminder that Hollywood has enough talent to produce unforgettable images just about any time it wants to.

'*Hard Rain* has what the other disaster flicks that keep spilling out of tabloid land don't have: a real story line, shades of good and bad and grey, the everyday evils of human beings played out against the force of nature, and people you actually care about. There isn't a bad actor here. Asner is outstanding in his short stint. Freeman, as always, is the consummate professional. Randy Quaid gives what may be his best performance since *The Last Detail*. And Michael Goorjian deserves praise for the shadings he gives to a slow-witted robber.

'Christian is far too cool, way too quick-thinking, and stubbornly good-looking through it all, even when he's drenched and wheezing. And Minnie Driver, bright and feisty and believably Midwestern, can do no wrong. Both of them are brave and bold and true. When they're hiding inside a car being crushed by the flood, with people intent on killing them all around, they're spouting happy-face talk, making jokes about a *Footloose* tape. But that's to be expected in this kind of flick, where you're not allowed to think about anything seriously for more than thirty seconds.

'If you thought about it too long, you'd find it laughable that a major dam in a flooded area would have only one man on the job, and that he would leave when the storm was at its worst. You'd laugh at guns working perfectly after lying under water for hours. You'd wonder why people who got shot don't seem to be wounded at all, and you'd howl at some sleazo getting babe-hungry in the middle of a shootout and a flood that's eating houses alive.

'But *Hard Rain*, at a fast ninety-eight minutes, doesn't allow you to think about it. It wants you to sit there with your mouth open, popcorn dribbling from your hand, giving a nod to the good acting, the excellent cinematography, the fine stunt work and incredible special effects.

'And it wants you to lock in on the set, a meticulous re-creation of the real town of Huntingburg, in a former B-1 bomber factory, flooded by five million gallons of water, drizzled in a constant rain back-lit by floodlights, crisscrossed by speeding boats and jet skis and people popping out of the water at the craziest times. From beginning to end, *Hard Rain* wants you to marvel at what your eyes are seeing. And you know what? You do.'

Interestingly, it was in an interview to promote the film for

Cosmopolitan magazine that Christian was described as now being all grown up: 'Unlike the old days of serial girlfriends, arrest for driving under the influence, and angry attacks on directors he didn't like and parents who did him wrong, the twenty-seven-year-old actor now shows up on time, refuses to speak against the people he works with and instead talks quietly of being loved by his father, supported by his mother, in love with his work and enchanted with his little half-brother, Ryan [fourteen years his junior from Mary Jo's second marriage to lawyer and estate agent William Taron].' But perhaps that was all down to the fact that he'd got to know himself better. 'I got perspective,' he observed. 'It's OK to just be me.'

The idea of Christian being 'far too cool', though, was a criticism that appeared to follow him in every one of his movies since *Heathers* and *Pump Up the Volume*. Britain's *Film Review* magazine posed exactly the same question when they caught up with Christian just before he was heading off to prison, asking, 'Isn't he going to be playing the same smart alec that we're so used to seeing him play?'

No, argued Christian. 'I got to be involved in it from the early, early stages, having a relationship with Mark Gordon and Graham Yost from *Broken Arrow*,' he discloses. 'That's how I got the credit of co-producer – just being in a room with them and for a couple of months, developing the script and ideas. I didn't want to be a smartass character. I wanted it to be a more grown-up guy, but a good guy. A decent guy.'

Sharing the same view of the movie as that professed by the *San Francisco Examiner*'s movie reviewer, he continues, 'I think *Hard Rain* is the kind of movie that has so many twists and turns. It's got these great characters and there's a real storyline. It's not just a disaster movie; there's a lot going on, and you're never quite sure who the bad guy is. Just when you think you know what's happening, something changes. I think that keeps the audience on the edge of their seats. The fact that we've got this threat of Mother Nature coming down on us all the time adds quite a few elements to it that makes it an exciting, breathtaking, suffocating, wet and wild ride.'

Part of that excitement, as far as Christian was concerned, was the fact that there were no special effects, no bluescreen trickery or computer animation used to create the rising water. Instead, the back-to-basics film-makers moved into a hangar the size of three football fields at Rockwell International's facility in Palmdale, California, built a huge tank and filled it with five million gallons of water heated to a comfortable 85°F. The sets were then placed on top of the water and lowered into it to simulate the rising level of the flood.

There wasn't one day of shooting when Christian and his co-stars weren't wet. 'It was cold sometimes,' he confessed. 'It was miserable. There were scenes with me and Minnie Driver where she and I are floating down the street in this car and the water's up to our necks, but we were actually happy that we're in the car because at least we're out of the simulated rain.' It was, Christian repeats, 'a unique experience'.

At one point in the film, Christian's character is trapped in a jail cell slowly filling with water after a levee has broken. In reality, though, the cell is descending into the bathlike tank. Even though he knew he was safe and under water for only seconds at a time – long enough to shoot each take – he could well imagine the panic of drowning.

'When the water actually comes over your head, there's nothing you can do!'

However, Christian took steps to confront his fear, earning certification as a diver after taking scuba lessons on the weekends during shooting. 'I went on this 80ft-deep-wreck dive in the British Virgin Islands, to this old ship called *The Roan*,' he recalled. 'It was just incredible, swimming around this hull. It couldn't be more peaceful. You're encased in this underwater world. The only thing you can hear is your breathing. Beautiful. When you find heaven on earth, it just makes this business a lot easier to take, because you know that it exists.'

If there was any doubt about the timing for the release of the movie in America or Britain, Christian wasn't too bothered. Although he had thoughts of 'running and bailing', as he puts it, the truth was that he'd become addicted to fear. 'It feels much better. A lot of people either run away and don't necessarily face what they need to face. Then the problems grow and end up eating your soul. This has been an incredible opportunity for me to take responsibility and accept the consequences. I'm doing everything I can in the best possible way I can.'

Although by the time he made these comments his drug and alcohol abuse had been extensively recorded over the previous months in almost every journal one could think of, Christian was still evasive about the extent of his imprisonment. 'I'm not really prepared at this point to discuss what the problems are,' he said cagily. 'I can't really go into that. The irony of this situation is that *Hard Rain* pretty much prepared me for any horrors that you might face in real life. I definitely went through a lot of situations being in five million gallons of water and having 30,000 gallons of water pouring down on my head.'

The buzz surrounding *Hard Rain* didn't spring from Christian's performance, however, but from the fact that he was serving out jail time during the film's release. 'I spent fifty-nine days sitting in a cell. I was stripped of all bullshit and all labels other than trustee,' he told *Heat* magazine two years later when they caught up with him for an interview. He even gave the publication a weekly run-down on his daily routine inside: 'Wake up, make breakfast, lunch, dinner. It was jail food, not pretty to look at. I'd prepare that stuff for prisoners they would arrest that night. Make sure the cells were clean. Mopping, sweeping, dusting, cooking, cleaning up the puke from the drunks who were in there the night before. It was disgusting. Unpleasant. Not fun. It was not cool.

'I was a criminal among criminals. I was in jail; I was doing time. Nobody treated me any differently. Nobody cared. I was fortunate that I was given writing materials, that I could read and listen to tapes.'

According to others, however, his time inside wasn't quite that tough. Sure, he might have had to share his cell with up to three other inmates and spend the bulk of his time preparing and serving meals, washing police cars, cleaning toilets and mopping floors, but what he didn't mention was the fact that his cell was furnished with a television, video recorder and telephone, that he brought his own clothes and bed linen, that he could entertain visitors on Sundays, that he could choose whether to eat jail food or have his own delivered, and that he had free use of the facility's microwave and fridge. And in his list of daily chores he neglected to include the painting and gardening he did.

And, then, fifty-nine days after starting his ninety-day sentence, he was released on good behaviour. According to one reporter, 'About thirty fans gathered outside the LA Verne Public Safety Facility in California – also known as the city jail – to welcome Slater back to society. The actor's attorney, who brought Slater clean clothes, told the crowd that his client was happy to be free. Minutes later, a visibly delighted Slater emerged with a triumphant roar. He was so psyched that he drove around the block several times before heading off.'

All the same, Christian still had to enter mandatory in-patient rehab for an additional ninety days, pay $1,300 in restitution, keep away from the victims of the outburst that landed him in jail in the first place, take an AIDS test, attend mandatory AIDS education classes and undergo a year-long course of treatment as a batterer. However, even though it would still be some months before he truly figured out what was what, he knew that he was finally on the road to recovery.

Chapter 11

Back To Basics

By October 1998, Christian was back in New York after deciding to return to Broadway theatre to appear in Warren Leight's *Side Man*, a play that, according to *The New York Times*, had been on a veritable walking tour of Manhattan. The production's unusual journey began in the spring of 1998 with a brief but acclaimed run in a little off-Broadway theatre and continued with a successful move for the summer to the main stage of the normally revival-driven Roundabout Theater Company.

By the time Christian joined it, the show had become quite an abnormality in that it had become commercially successful on Broadway, traditionally the home of musicals. Uprooting a new straight production to play there was a dangerous proposition because the organisers couldn't count on the musical-devouring tourist trade or on the kind of built-in hype that often attends a glittery London transfer.

Certainly, at the time it opened, the survival of *Side Man* depended on a smaller, specialised audience of serious theatregoers.

To those who saw it, *Side Man* was a tender, deeply personal memory play about the turmoil of a jazz musician's family as his career crumbles at the dawn of the age of rock 'n' roll. Seeing the action unfold on a big stage was something like peering at Broadway through his giant stereopticons of ragtime, serving as a gentle reminder of bygone days when a new play by William Inge or Tennessee Williams would stir up the public and fill seats for months.

In its depiction of a young man struggling to remain the glue in the troubled marriage of his vacant, trumpet-playing father and unbalanced, alcoholic mother, *Side Man* has an abiding power, although of a muted variety. As most critics agreed, anyone who was going to see the play expecting *tour de force* portrayals or actorly pyrotechnics would more likely feel as if they'd walked into the wrong neighbourhood. The word around Broadway was 'unmissable'.

Directed by Michael Mayer, the production was, according to New York critic Peter Marks, practically a mirror of its Roundabout incarnation, but with one important exception: 'the addition of the movie actor Christian Slater in the central role of Clifford, the play's put-upon son and narrator'. Christian had stepped in to replace Robert Stella, the role's originator, who had left to fill in for Alan Cumming as the MC in *Cabaret*.

In his review of the production, Mayer continued, 'Slater's performance is courageously economical and without showiness; it retains the actor's cinematic sense of containment in close-up. This works extremely well in a role that is all about the witnessing, absorbing and denying of pain. His composure pays off remarkably at the play's subtle climax, when Clifford must thoroughly assume the role of parent to his parents and cast his ineffectual father, Gene (played by Frank Wood), out of the family's apartment. The actor never overplays Clifford's festering anger. It's expressed, in fact, only once, when Gene suggests that he has no responsibility for the pathetic condition of his wife, Terry (Wendy Makkena), now confined to a psychiatric hospital. Disgusted, Slater sends Wood flying helplessly into a chair. Suddenly aware of his power, and inclined to use it, the son has taken control. Slater pulls this off so unself-consciously that you believe in it as an act of frustrated love rather than rage.

'Alternating between the family's apartment and Gene's world of versatile, freelance jazz musicians – the side men of the title – the play conjures an extremely specific slice of New York City between 1953 and 1985. It pairs the story of the decline of jazz with the disintegration of Clifford's family and in some of the moodier interludes erupt with a astonishing joy, as when, in flashback, Gene woos Terry with a bluesy trumpet version of Debussy. But no moment is better than the one in which Gene, sitting with two of his cronies, played delightfully by Michael Mastro and Joseph Lyle Taylor, is swept away listening to a cassette of a heartache-filled trumpet solo. Wood's rapture is even more wrenching than the music.'

Clive Barnes, reviewing the production in the *New York Post*, was equally enthusiastic, gushing about how Christian adds more than just a little clout. He had no doubt that

Christian himself 'would be the first to admit that this is essential to an ensemble play, and Slater's role as Clifford, although the autobiographical key to this memory play, is not any more important than at least two of the other characters, Clifford's parents. But that said, Slater, who has not had a great deal of previous stage experience, fits in with the rest of the production and Michael Mayer's subtly persuasive staging ideally just as he should. His wry, very ironic, even slightly embittered presence strikes the right note, while the rest of the cast remains among the best ensembles to light up Broadway in years.'

When Christian appeared at a party to celebrate the success of *Side Man*, he revealed publicly something that the tabloid press had been insisting on for a few weeks: that he and Kim Walker, his co-star from *Heathers* and the girlfriend he supposedly left for Winona Ryder, were back together. Although the couple retained a reasonably low profile and claimed to be just good friends, the *New York Daily* published a report that alleged there was more to it than that. To complicate matters even more, Christian refused to let photographers take any pictures of them together, even when Walker again accompanied him to the opening of the show after he had left the production.

Perhaps this was just tabloid tittle-tattle, however. Certainly, when Christian attended the opening of his latest movie, *Very Bad Things*, just one week later, it was without Walker. Although his new film had already been premiered at the Toronto Film Festival that September, it was Christian's first movie since he was released from prison to strike a profitable chord with audiences and the box office.

Christian at the Festival Du Film De Paris Tribute in April 2000. Christian was honoured at the tribute alongside Rosanna Arquette.

Above left: Christian on holiday with wife Ryan Haddon in Porto Cervo, Italy, June 2004.

Above Right: Christian, Ryan and children, Jaden and Elaina, at the premiere of *The Incredibles* at the Empire Theatre in Leicester Square, London in November 2004.

Below: Christian with Ryan at the premiere of Johnny Depp's *Finding Neverland* in London, October 2004.

Above: Christian and co-star Neve Campbell filming *Churchill: The Hollywood Years* at the Royal William Yard in Plymouth, April 2003.

Below: Christian with Neve during a break in filming.

Playing Randle P McMurphy in the Edinburgh and London stage version of
Ken Kesey's *One Flew Over The Cuckoo's Nest*, was a dream Christian held ever
since watching his idol Jack Nicholson play the same part in the 1975 film version.

Above: Christian, Frances Barber and MacKenzie Crook during rehearsals for
One Flew Over The Cuckoo's Nest at the Garrick Theatre in London, July 2004

Below: Christian signing autographs for fans during his stay in Britain while starring
in the stage version of *One Flew Over The Cuckoo's Nest.*

Christian with his mother, and now manager, Mary Jo Slater at the opening night party of *The Glass Menagerie* in New York, 22 March 2005.

Christian and Nicolas Cage accompanied their *Windtalkers* director John Woo for his hand and footprint ceremony at Mann's Chinese Theatre in downtown Hollywood in May 2002.

Christian at the Broadway Show League Softball Season Opening Day in
Central Park, New York on 5 May 2005.

Very Bad Things relates the story of how, during a raucous bachelor party, the death of a Las Vegas stripper sets off a murderous chain reaction that exposes the savagery and rage hidden beneath the placid surface of conventional suburban life. Besides being darkly hilarious, the film was also, quite unexpectedly, a moral tale that explored the dangers of wedding-day hysteria and the scarier aspects of male bonding. It was, writer Peter Berg explained, a movie that 'takes place during the final week of a wedding and [describes] how the groomsmen become involved in a sort of homicidal episode which, like a bad red-wine stain, refuses to come out'.

Film critic Roger Ebert, however, was unconvinced. What bothered him most, after two viewings, was the film's confidence that 'an audience would be entertained by its sad, sick vision, tainted by racism. If this material had been presented straight, as a drama, the movie would have felt more honest and might have been more successful. Its cynicism is the most unattractive thing about it, the assumption that an audience has no moral limits and will laugh at cruelty simply to feel hip. I know moral detachment is a key element of the ironic pose, but there is a point, once reached, which provides a test of your underlying values.'

The story of the film, from Peter Berg's own script, centred on five lifelong buddies: a real-estate agent named Robert Boyd (Christian); the quiet and shy mechanic Charles Moore (Leland Orser); Kyle Fisher (Jon Favreau), whose imminent betrothal to the marriage-obsessed Laura (Cameron Diaz) is the very reason for the party in the first place; and antagonist brothers Adam (Daniel Stern) and

Michael Berkow (Jeremy Piven), who travel to Vegas to celebrate Fisher's last days of freedom. Even though the idea for them all is a chance to rage wildly and behave like adolescents, things soon go badly wrong.

When the bachelor party kicks off, everything seems to be going according to plan, with all the usual ingredients for such get-togethers: booze, drugs, loud music, drunken antics, broken furniture and a stripper. There is a problem, however, with the stripper – or, at least, with what happens to her. After she lap dances with most of the guys, she is steered by Michael into the bathroom, where he lurches drunkenly about her until her head is accidentally impaled on a coat hook. A few minutes later, Michael emerges from the bathroom covered in blood and the stripper lies dead on the marble floor. While brother Adam and Michael quarrel over responsibility and Kyle freaks out, bad boy Boyd takes charge of the situation and forbids them to call the police. 'Take away the horror of the situation. Take away the tragedy of her death. Take away all the moral and ethical considerations you have had drummed into you since childhood and what are you left with? A hundred-and-five-pound problem.'

Michael, however, has a solution: cut her up and bury her in the Nevada desert. He browbeats the others into going along with his plan. Everything's going smoothly until a security guard enters, following up a complaint about noise levels, and catches glimpse of the dead body, which forces Robert to stab the guard with a corkscrew. Now there are two bodies to dispose of, and from that point on the rest of the movie is, as Roger Ebert explains, a 'stride though a hardware store like *Reservoir Dogs*'. In no time at all, friend is pitted against friend, brother against brother and husband against wife as the boys try to clean up the mess while a determined and increasingly psychotic Laura battles to get through the week of marriage festivities that are now threatened by the homicidal savagery that has been unleashed.

Although it sounds like a horror film – and it is, in part – the movie was very comical, according to those involved in its making. Jeanne Tripplehorn, who plays Adam's wife, Lois, had stated unreservedly that it was 'just the darkest comedy I've ever read. It is so dark, and the things that happen are so tragic, that after a while you have to laugh.' Daniel Stern had much the same view. 'One of the things that I found really funny is that, right in the middle of these horrible moments, something inane catches my character's attention. We're standing over a corpse, burying her chopped-up body, and we have an argument as to whether I have any friends. That kind of juxtaposition I think is surprising and funny.'

Like that of *Heathers* before it, the script of *Very Bad Things* certainly had some dark parts that made people squirm, but it was still a rollercoaster ride. As producer Cindy Cowan insisted, 'It's weird, it's wild, it's funny, it's intense, it's strange. It's the darkest of comedies.'

Although in part *Very Bad Things* was a film about the hysteria and determination surrounding a wedding day, Berg reasons, 'Weddings are so stress-producing that it's not completely out of reason that the wedding parties become so involved with the pageantry of a wedding that they actually start killing themselves to make sure the wedding goes off as planned.'

Cameron Diaz, Christian's co-star in *Very Bad Things*, was

equally enthralled. In her explanation of her character's motivation, she echoes Berg's observation: 'Laura is an average girl whose one ambition in life is to get married. She's dreamed of this day, and she's incredibly determined to do it. I think she's threatened by her husband's buddies in that they're always trying to take up his time, the time she wants. All those guys seem to think that that's what boys do, but these guys are something else.'

As Jon Favreau, who plays Laura's husband, also explains, 'Any good film is allegorical for the turmoil that goes on inside someone's head when they're about to make a decision. And getting married is a big step; there's lots of anxiety.'

In *Very Bad Things*, the counterpart to the stress caused by wedding-day expectations is the murky psychology of male bonding, which Berg acknowledges is what interested him most. In the story, he took normal people – 'guys that pay their credit-card bills, people that went to college, drive sensible cars, don't speed – and introduces them into a world of gruesome horror and sees how each one of them responded'.

Perhaps even more interesting is the fact that it was Berg's visits to Las Vegas that gave him the idea for the script in the first place. 'I would see these packs of guys, bombed out of their minds, just raging. And what always amazed me is how much repression was in these guys. They would engage in the ritual of getting together in Vegas and animalistic urges and animalistic behaviour would come out.'

Co-producer Michael Schiffer, meanwhile, remarked that, if nothing else, the movie is the story of 'the dissolution of the Western world as we know it, where five guys revert to primitive. You can't help but laugh, because it's so demented. Christian lays the blame on the character he plays. This guy is just so insane – I mean, the guy is the Devil – and he gets surrounded by a group of guys that are willing to follow him.'

Christian attributes the bad behaviour exhibited by the film's characters to their being confronted by a crazy and unanticipated situation. Throw in drugs and a demonic leader and you get some very bad things indeed. 'They're never completely innocent,' he notes, 'and as a result of one night of total debauchery their whole existence changes. It's just not always good to listen to the Devil.'

Despite the story's strange and twisted nature, the general consensus of both cast and crew was that it contains some valuable lessons. Leland Orser was one of those who found a 'terrible beauty and a terrible tragedy' in the film, partly because it explores what happens when you face death and, whether in extreme circumstance or not, 'you turn *to* your friends or turn *on* your friends'.

As Orser continues to explain, 'It's how the American dream turns into the American nightmare. But the moral of the story is don't do very bad things or there will be consequences for your action. You will indeed reap what you sow in a major way.'

Perhaps for Christian the redeeming value of Berg's film is that audiences will 'look at films like this and experiences like this as little learnings that, hopefully, we don't have to go through'. In fact, Christian suspects that *Very Bad Things* will make people think twice about bachelor parties just as much as the movie *Fatal Attraction* made people think twice about having affairs.

Not everyone, of course, completely shared Roger Ebert's view of the film. The film's reviewer in the *San Francisco Chronicle*, for instance, reported, 'It may be silly and superficial, but it is lively and undeniably entertaining. If Berg were a worse writer with no dramatic instincts, he'd have tried to pass this nonsense off as serious – and been rewarded by great reviews from gullible critics. To his credit, he pitched it to the vulgar masses – the right and honest thing to do with a vulgar movie.'

Vulgar or not, the question on everyone's lips was, how difficult was it for Christian to work on a film that featured drugs and alcohol, the very same things that got him locked up? Even if it bothered him, Christian, of course, didn't let on, responding, 'I really saw it as an opportunity to observe, to be on the outside and be sober and totally aware of a lot of insanity. It gave me a real bird's-eye view of the beast.' Even in the scenes depicting people snorting cocaine, Christian affirms that he wasn't that bothered: 'I really wasn't part of those scenes, but I had one of those Vicks inhalers. That kind of cleared out my nasal passages and gave me a rush.'

Looking back, however – and in view of his own colourful past – perhaps it wasn't so surprising that Christian accepted the role in the film. 'The reason the movie worked for me was that my character tells these guys it's all going to be fine, but then during the course of the movie you see how, when you try to cover something up, it's going to blow up in your face,' he observed. 'I see it as a black comedy: it's very dark, sick, risky. It's a bachelor party – Vegas; there's a hooker there; there's drugs, booze – all the elements that lead to disaster. I know about this. I've been there; I've lived it. I mean, I wasn't stabbing people with corkscrews, as my character does, but definitely there were similarities. This guy was the dark side of me. I got to play that character and then I got to go back to my trailer and I didn't have to be that guy.'

However, Christian also acknowledges, somewhat carefully, 'I've been in situations where I've had to make choices – just deciding whether to tell the truth and come clean when others were trying to convince me otherwise. But I got tired of creating stories; it just got too exhausting. It got so agonisingly painful to come up with one more story. I can't do it any more. I have told so many lies – big, medium, and minuscule – my conscience won't allow me to do it any more.'

After having said that, however, he still had no idea why men engage in the kind of behaviour detailed in the film – 'Who knows? Men are idiots. Men are goofs' – and, although he enjoyed making the film, showing up every day and giving 100 per cent, he has never used the kind of self-help manuals pored over by Robert Boyd in the movie, although he did read a couple for research purposes. 'One said you should imagine what you'd feel like if you had a cape on,' he recalled, 'and it felt really good, in a bizarre, psychotic kind of way.'

Even when asked how much of himself he put into the self-styled vaguely demonic Boyd, he replied, 'It's certainly a particular side to me. There were qualities there that I could relate to, but it kind of gave me a chance to draw a really clear line between the kind of person I'd like to be and the kind of person I don't want to be. We all have the ability to be axe murderers or Buddhists; it just depends what kind of mood you wake up in. I moved out to Los Angeles when I was sixteen and I've been on a search for an identity of my own, figuring out who I really want to be. And, if you start out in this business and you don't have that foundation, it gets dangerous.'

After *Very Bad Things* had done the rounds, Christian wasn't seen on the big screen again for nearly two years, and only then in a supporting role.

Chapter 12

From The White House to Graceland

If Christian had been encouraged by the critical reaction to *Very Bad Things*, he would remain equally pleased by the reviews for his next major screen role, in *The Contender*, a film rooted in the tradition of *All the President's Men*, *The Candidate* and *The Seduction of Joe Tynan*. A political thriller that goes behind the scenes of political power plays, *The Contender* tells the story of the first woman nominated to be Vice-President, whose candidacy hinges on a question from her past: did she more or less willingly participate in group sex while she was in college? 'That's Hanson getting gang-banged,' an investigator says, smacking his lips over an old photo from a sorority party. If it really is, she's going to have trouble getting congressional confirmation.

The only problem with the film was that many thought it to be rather biased and opinionated. Its sentiments, noted film critic Roger Ebert, 'are liberal and Democratic, its villains conservative and Republican'. Even when the reviewer asked its star, Jeff Bridges, whether the plot was a veiled reference to Monicagate, the actor confessed that he didn't think so. If anything, he mused, "'The difference between Senator Laine Hanson (Joan Allen) and President Clinton is that, when zealots start sniffing her laundry, she simply refuses to answer their questions. 'It's none of your business,' she tells GOP Rep. Shelly Runyon (Gary Oldman), whose inquiring mind wants to know.'"

Indeed, at the film's opening it transpires that an incumbent Vice-President has died in office, and it's universally assumed that the man to replace him will be Governor Jack Hathaway (William Petersen), who has recently made headlines as a hero, attempting (unsuccessfully) to rescue a woman trapped in a car in icy waters. It is apparently an adventure like this, not a lifetime of service, that the image-mongers like. However, the governor's misfortune is that his rescue attempt failed. 'A girl died, and you let it happen,' he's told sorrowfully by presidential advisers, but President Jackson Evans (Jeff Bridges) consoles him cryptically, 'You're the future of the Democratic Party, and you always will be.'

In Hathaway's place, President Evans wants to make history by appointing a woman, and he thinks the best choice is Senator Hanson, who is happily married with a young child, and who, when we first see her, is having robust sex on a desktop with her husband. Republican Congressman Shelly Runyon, however, doubts that any woman should be trusted with the nuclear trigger. After all, what if she has her period or something? He is simply delighted when evidence turns up suggesting that she might have been the life of the party on campus.

Senator Hanson, however, flatly refuses to answer any questions about her sexual past, and for a time it looks as if the President might have to dump her as a nominee. Is she really taking an ethical stand, or is she covering up something? There is a remarkable scene featuring Hanson and Runyon having lunch together in a private club, the Republican shovelling down his meal and talking with his mouth full as if he would like to chew on her, too.

Most American movies pretend that US politics is non-partisan; even in political movies, characters rarely reveal their affiliations. In *The Contender*, however, the political view of each character is revealed, most obviously that of GOP Representative Runyon as an unprincipled power-broker with an unwholesome curiosity about other people's sex lives.

Whether or not audiences were in sympathy with the movie depended largely on which they found more disturbing: the questions posed by the Starr Commission or Clinton's attempts to avoid answering them. One can imagine that most would perhaps react as Clinton did, but to ask Starr's questions would probably have filled most people with self-disgust. As Ebert pointed out, 'Joan Allen is at the centre of *The Contender*, in one of the strongest performances of the year. Some actresses would have played the role as too sensual, others as too cold; she is able to suggest a woman with a healthy physical life who nevertheless has ethical standards that will not bend. She would rather lose the vice-presidency than satisfy Runyon's smutty curiosity and, through her, the movie argues that we have gone too far in our curiosity about private behaviour.

'Jeff Bridges plays the President as a man who got elected by seeming a great deal more affable and downhome than he really is. He's forever ordering food and pressing it upon his guests, in gestures that are not so much hospitality as decoys. His top aides, played by Sam Elliott and Saul Rubinek, have a terse shorthand that shows they understand the folksy act but aren't deceived by it. And Christian Slater has a slippery role as a freshman Democratic Representative who is prepared to barter his vote for a seat on Runyon's committee.

'And what about Runyon, in Gary Oldman's performance? Oldman is one of the great actors, able to play high, low, crass, noble. Here he disappears into the character, with owly glasses, a feral mouth and curly locks teased over baldness. He plays the kind of man who, in high school, would rather know who was sleeping with the cheerleaders than sleep with one himself. There are two revealing scenes involving his wife, who knows him better than anyone should have to. Of course, if he is right about Hanson, then he is not a bad man, merely an unpleasant one. But even if he is right, he is wrong, because he opposed the nominee because she is a woman; her shady past is only a means of attacking her. This is one of those rare movies where you leave the theatre having been surprised and entertained, and then start arguing.'

A self-described political junkie, writer and director Rod Lurie admitted that he enjoys the power plays of government and that Monicagate was the inspiration behind the movie. 'Presidential election years are like football seasons to me,' he said. 'I watch the events unfold with great excitement. I can't wait to see who the Vice-Presidential pick will be. I can't wait to see the debates.'

As a former film critic and entertainment journalist, Lurie also revealed his affinity for movies with political backdrops, especially those that give audiences an insider's view of the manipulation and machinations of power. 'In the 1970s, we had films like *All the President's Men*, *The Candidate* and *The Parallax View*. I loved them, even as a little boy. The political films of recent years are more satires. With *The Contender*, I tried to do something different, more of a throwback to those earlier movies.'

Certainly, the film was more about principles than politics. 'The challenges that Senator Laine Hanson faces in this film are decidedly more about her personal life than her public persona,' Lurie observed. 'Her principles tell her that under no circumstance should she allow her personal life to mesh with her public one, and her courageousness emerges when she takes a stand and refuses to give in, despite pressure from both sides. Her heroics are based on her sticking to those principles even when they're inconvenient.'

Even so, while the situation described in *The Contender* might have arisen from Lurie's fascination with politics, he has no hesitation in revealing that it was written specifically for the award-winning actress who stars as Senator Laine Hanson: Joan Allen. 'I did more than write this movie with Joan in mind for the role of Laine Hanson; I wrote the movie itself for her. I am a gigantic fan of hers. I think she is quite simply the best actress in the world.'

Interestingly, Lurie's decision to write the script was

initiated by an off-the-cuff remark the screenwriter made while presenting Allen with a Los Angeles Film Critics' Award for her work in Gary Ross's 1998 *Pleasantville.* 'I got up on the stage and, impromptu, said, "I should write a screenplay for Joan Allen,"' he remembered. 'When I sat down with her afterwards, she told me to write that screenplay. Joan has never played a character which an entire movie revolves on, and that's what I wanted to give her, so the role of Laine Hanson was born.'

Allen was understandably flattered to have the central role of the film written specifically for her, but she was even more thrilled upon reading the script. 'I thought it was really wonderful,' she recalled. 'It's a dream for an actor to have a role like this, but the whole script is so good. And all the characters in it are terrific, not just mine.'

In fact, Allen had been filming in Ireland when she was first handed the screenplay of *The Contender*, but immediately upon her return she immersed herself in what Lurie teasingly calls a 'research frenzy'. 'I studied the script and tried to chart Hanson's emotional life,' Allen recalled. 'We had the great luxury of rehearsing for two weeks, so Rod and I were able to discuss and refine our ideas for the character. I was extremely fortunate to know a lot about Laine's past – that she's the daughter of a governor and was raised in a political world, and at some point had switched parties.

'I think she feels smart and savvy enough to handle the situation because she understands the Washington scene. It's been her life for so many years. But she also has an underlying conviction that her personal life has no place in the political process. She believes it with all her heart and just can't operate any other way. I think it would certainly be easier for her to capitulate, but it's not in her make-up, so she just digs in her heels. Her principles are unshakeable. That's a valuable quality to have, which is something the President comes to recognise in her.'

Equally thrilled to be cast was Jeff Bridges, recruited to play President Jackson Evans, whose choice of a woman to become his new Vice-President leads to a showdown on Capitol Hill. 'I've spent some time in Washington, lobbying for different causes, and I'd always thought it would be interesting to play someone in politics,' he admitted, 'but to play the President of the United States is an entirely different matter. It was fascinating to get in touch with that kind of power and what a complex job it is, but then you have to put it in some kind of normal context. There has to be a seeming normalcy to your portrayal, because that is his everyday life.'

Certainly, most critics agreed that the brilliance of Jeff Bridges is his subtlety. As Lurie pointed out, 'I wrote the character of President Evans a lot more cut and dried than what Jeff actually brought to the screen. With Jeff, you don't really know what Evans's motivations are for putting a woman in the office of Vice-President, or his reasoning for sticking by Laine Hanson so strongly.'

'It's virtually impossible in politics to paint anyone as a good guy or a bad guy,' Lurie continued. 'The notion of what is good and what is bad changes with time. It's not just liberal versus conservative; it's not just good versus bad. Human beings tend to be enigmas, and social or political ideologies should represent that. If you look at the character of Congressman Shelly Runyon, he's ostensibly the bad guy, but that depends on his motives. If he truly feels that Laine Hanson is the wrong person for the job, then it's merely his tactics that are questionable and not what's in his heart. Runyon is an old-style politician. His only concerns are his constituency, the US Congress and what he sees as what's best for the country, and he's a master at steering people on the issues he cares about. Gary, for one, never believed his character was in any way the villain of the movie, which might seem confounding to some people, but he did feel he had discovered Runyon's motivation and really understood why he was doing what he was doing. He gained enormous empathy for Runyon.'

Indeed, as Oldman noted, 'Shelly is very much of the old school, but he knows there's this whole thing today of having to be PC. It's about going out there and putting on the mask – there's the public face and the backstage, private face. I think you get a delicious mix of the two in this film. You're taken behind the scenes in a very interesting way. It was a great part and a really smart script. I just wasn't sure I was old enough for the role the way it was written.'

In addition to the age difference between Oldman and the character he plays, there's also the fact that the actor is British, although anyone who has followed his career shouldn't be surprised at his ability to master a Midwestern American accent. However, in *The Contender* he is almost unrecognisable behind glasses and with a pronounced receding hairline. 'I'll never forget the first day he showed up on the set as Shelly,' remembered Lurie. 'I hadn't seen the look before and I was blown away. In fact, when he walked across the set, no one knew it was Gary Oldman.'

In the film, Christian played Reginald Webster, a young freshman Congressman whose character provides a foil for Oldman's elder statesman. 'Webster's a young man looking to get ahead,' observed Christian. 'He believes he's on the right side, but I don't think he's too particular at that point; he just wants to make the right connections. He is being moulded as the story progresses. His foundation isn't too solid to begin with, but over the course of events he sees things and develops some true beliefs of his own and begins to incorporate them into his behaviour. He's a much more solid person by the end.'

Although many of *The Contender*'s cast had worked together previously, the most interesting prior association belonged to Christian, who had played opposite Oldman in *True Romance* and, before that, almost at the beginning of his film career, had portrayed the son of Jeff Bridges and Joan Allen in *Tucker: The Man and his Dream*. 'It's amazing to look back on that,' he reflected. 'I was a completely different person then – this wild and crazy kid. It was great to be able to collaborate with them as contemporaries now.'

If some were disappointed with not seeing more of Christian in *The Contender*, they didn't have long to wait for a more decisive appearance. Four months later, he joined Kevin Costner and Kurt Russell in *3,000 Miles To Graceland*, a film that, according the *San Francisco Chronicle*'s Peter Stack, was 'an overstuffed, underfed numbskull movie of Elvis Presley lookalikes who knock over a Las Vegas casino during an Elvis convention. With all its potential for camp and glitz, and even some intelligence, this movie should have been a romp. Instead, it's a tedious caper saga of ultra-violent macho gunk, apparently aimed at pea brains.'

Roger Ebert didn't like the film, either. As far as he was concerned, it didn't have an ounce of human kindness, and was in general 'a sour and mean-spirited enterprise so desperate to please, it tries to be a yucky comedy and a hard-boiled action picture at the same time'. He took particular exception to a scene depicting the robbery of a casino, which, he reported, 'involves a gory bloodbath, all gratuitous, all intercut with an Elvis revue on one of the show stages. Not intercut a little, but a lot, complete with dancing girls, until we see so much of the revue we prefer it to the shooting. The gang makes off with the loot, there is the inevitable squabble over how to divvy it up, and then the movie's most intriguing and inexplicable relationship develops. This is between Kurt Russell and Courtney Cox, who plays the mom of a bright young kid (David Kaye) and is stranded in the Last Chance Motel, one of those movie sets from a Road Runner cartoon.

'Cox's character is intriguing because we never understand her motivation, and inexplicable because she doesn't, either. She really does like Russell, I guess, and that explains why they're in the sack so quickly, but then the kid, who is about eight, creeps into the bedroom and steals Russell's wallet. The movie never questions the wisdom of showing the kid in the room while his mother is in bed with a stranger. One imagines that the film-makers were so tickled by the plot point that the moral questions just didn't occur to them.

'At a point later in the movie, the Cox character drives off in a car containing most of Russell's loot while leaving her son behind with him. Would a mother do this? Some would, but most movies wouldn't consider them heroines. There is an "explanation" for her behaviour, based on the fact that Russell, a criminal she has known for about ten minutes, is obviously a good guy and she likes the guy – but, come on.

'The plot is standard double-reverse, post-*Reservoir Dogs* irony, done with a lot of style and a minimum of thought. It's about behaviour patterns, not personalities. Everybody is defined by what they do – or what they drive; as the film opens, Russell is in a 1957 red Cadillac and Costner drives a Continental convertible of similar vintage, perhaps because they want to look like Elvis impersonators, but more likely because all characters in movies like this drive 1950s cars because modern ones are too small and wimpy.

'The cast stays top-drawer right down to the supporting roles. Kevin Pollack turns up as a federal marshal, Jon Lovitz is a money launderer, Ice-T is hired muscle. You guess they all liked the script. But the Russell and Costner characters are so burdened by the baggage of their roles that sometimes they just seem weary, and the energy mostly comes from Cox – and from the kid, who seems to be smarter than anyone else in the film, and about as experienced.'

Like most of the film's reviewers, Ebert hardly mentioned Christian's role as one of the Costner and Russell gang, and even worse was the general consensus that the movie was hardly worth bothering about. But Ebert, being Ebert, did give the film credit for having a terrific trailer. 'When a bad movie produces a great trailer, it's usually evidence that the raw materials were there for a good movie. I can imagine a blood-soaked caper movie involving Elvis disguises, a lonely tramp and her bright-eyed son, but it isn't this one.'

Contributing his own footnote to the Presley musical

legacy, a few years after the release of *3,000 Miles To Graceland* Christian singled out Elvis's 'A Little Less Conversation' as his all-time favourite track. 'I fell in love with Elvis, watching all his movies,' he admitted. 'He was the ultimate rebel. Very cool. He will always be the original king of rock 'n' roll. I can't imagine anyone taking his crown. At the end of the day, people do want a little less conversation and little more action. They're good rules to live by.'

Perhaps Christian's reverence for Elvis was behind the lines that Quentin Tarantino wrote for him in the opening sequence of *True Romance*, when, as Clarence Worley, Christian is sitting in a smoky cocktail bar in downtown Detroit trying to pick up an older woman. 'In *Jailhouse Rock*, he's everything rockabilly's about,' Christian observed in the movie. 'I mean, he *is* rockabilly: mean, surly, nasty, rude. In that movie, he couldn't give a fuck about anything except rocking and rolling, living fast, dying young and leaving a good-looking corpse. I love that scene where, after he's made it big, he's throwing a big cocktail party, and all these highbrows are there and he's singing, "Baby, you're so square … Baby, I don't care." Now, they got him dressed like a dick. He's wearing these stupid-looking pants and this horrible sweater. Elvis ain't no sweater boy. I even think they got him wearing penny loafers. Despite all that shit – all the highbrows at the party, the big house, the stupid clothes – he's still a rude-looking motherfucker. I'd watch that hillbilly and I'd want to be him so bad. Elvis looked good. I'm no fag, but Elvis was good-looking. He was fucking prettier than most women. I always said if I ever had to fuck a guy – I mean had to 'cause my life depended on it – I'd fuck Elvis.'

It was also alleged that *3,000 Miles To Graceland* was yet another movie in which Christian became involved with a co-star – in this case, Courtney Cox – although neither has ever suggested that they were anything more than good friends. Indeed, by the time the movie was playing across America, in late February 2001, Christian had been married to former television producer Ryan Haddon for over a year.

According to the press, the couple had met while hiking in Malibu in 1998, soon after Christian had been released from prison that March, and by the following week he had proposed to her. 'But she wasn't going to rush into anything,' Christian remembered, deciding that he was going to have to pull out all the stops to convince her to marry him. Although he had sworn off drink and drugs, Haddon remained wary that he would again succumb to the temptations of alcohol and drugs that had almost wrecked his career in the first place, and, although their relationship might be fun, she probably had no idea that Christian would pursue her for two years in order to tempt her down the aisle. Eventually, she consented to be his wife, and on 14 February 2000 she married Christian at the Four Seasons Hotel in Beverly Hills. The ceremony, in which Ryan wore an elegant charmeuse silk sheath with a draped bodice and sweeping train designed by Vera Wang, and Christian wore a black Armani tuxedo, was witnessed by 150 guests and, according to Christian's publicist, officiated by author Neale Donald Walsch. The couple's vows were taken from Walsch's book *Conversation With God: Book 3*, which was also one of the many books among Elvis Presley's personal collection of first editions.

The previous April, Ryan had given birth to her and Christian's first child, a son by the name of Jaden Christopher – coincidentally, the exact same forenames as Will and Jada Smith's youngest. It might have been these two events – marriage and fatherhood – that convinced Christian to become a born-again Christian during the making of *The Contender*, one of four movies cast by Christian's mother, Mary Jo. 'It's not an act,' affirmed Rod Lurie. 'It's all for real. He prays before each take, and you can just sense the difference in his whole demeanour.'

However, when *Men's Health* magazine in Britain caught up with Christian for a March 2005 interview, almost three years after the birth of his daughter Eliana Sophia, Christian was telling a slightly different story about religion, his marriage and parenthood. 'I'm not especially religious, and I'm not a big reader, but I really got into a book called *Conversations With God*. It's the first in a series of three books by Neale Donald Walsch that a friend gave me. There is a quote in there that says, "The fastest way to know who you are is to first know who you are not." That book helped me realise that, all the different people I've hung out with and the different experiences I've had, it's all been part of the process of discovering who it is I am. So, in a way, none of it has been a waste.

'It was actually through that book that I met my wife. I saw her at the gym and she was reading this book. It gave us something amazing to talk about straight away. I discovered later that she had told a friend, "Whatever man loves this book is the man I am going to marry." It was deep. We were both seriously into it. We read the whole series of books together, and there were some vows in there that were amazing. My wife wrote to the guy who wrote them, and he ended up marrying us. Our vows were beautiful. They weren't scary, with words like "obey" and "death". They were freeing and loving rather than suffocating.

'I'd never really envisaged myself as the marrying kind when I was younger. Marriage? Kids? Forget it! It did scare me, but it was just another one of those anxiety things to get through. Prior to becoming a father, I had to go through all these changes. If I were to have a child and not know who I was, that would really be unfortunate for the kid because he would have a dad who was unavailable, self-obsessed and lost. But now I can be there for both my kids.

'I was at the birth of both my children, Jaden and Eliana. I cut the cords, did the whole thing. I love them in so many ways. They're full of life and so much fun. Inevitably, I think having kids makes you settle down. It's a huge responsibility.'

Much more disappointing than what Christian was up to in his personal life was his next movie, *Who Is Cletis Tout?*, which was given only a limited release in America in the summer of 2002. As Roger Ebert noted, it was 'one of those movies with a plot so labyrinthine you think you should be taking notes and then you realise you are. Like *The Usual Suspects*, it circles around the verbal description of events that are seen in flashback and may or may not be trustworthy. The difference is that *Cletis Tout?* is a lot more lighthearted than the usual puzzle movie and takes its tone from the performance of Tim Allen, as Critical Jim, a hitman who loves the movies. As the film opens, he sticks a gun in the face of Christian Slater and tells him that in ninety minutes, if money isn't delivered as planned, he will kill him. In the meantime, he loves a good story. And Slater has one to tell him. Their meeting, Slater explains, is based on a misconception. Critical Jim thinks Slater is Cletis Tout, a man the mob wants dead, but Slater is in fact Trevor Finch, who borrowed Cletis Tout's identity after escaping from prison.

'Critical Jim cries, "Yes, I like flashbacks!" So Finch – if that is his name – tells a story about meeting a jewel thief named Micah (Richard Dreyfuss) in prison and learning from him about a stash of diamonds. Micah we have already seen; he is a gifted magician who stages his robbery while always seeming to be on the sidewalk outside the building. Later, in a prison break, he projects footage of himself against a background of smoke, which seems like a lot of trouble and leaves you wondering how a guy on a chain gang can smuggle a projector out to the work area.

'Anyway. Micah and Finch escape together (jumping on to a train that seems to be speeding way too fast), and then there is the business of the buried diamonds, and Micah's daughter Tess (Portia de Rossi), who either hates Finch or loves him, depending on various stages of the story. "Pitch me!" Critical Jim says, and Finch makes the story good while we try to decide what to believe.

'It's endearing, the way Critical Jim has memorised lines of movie dialogue to cover every occasion, but about midway through the movie I began to lose patience with the method, however clever. The underlying story about the original robbery, the jailbreak and the case of mistaken identity involving the mob is intriguing in itself. Add the beautiful Tess and her carrier pigeons (yes, carrier pigeons) and you have something. Is it entirely necessary to add the layer of the story being told to Critical Jim? Is this not one more unnecessary turn of the screw, to make a sound story into a gimmick? Could be. Or maybe not. By the end of the film I was a little restless, a little impatient at being jerked this way and that by the story devices. There was a lot I liked in *Cletis Tout?*, including the performances and the very audacity of details like the magic tricks and the carrier pigeons. But it seemed a shame that the writer and director, Chris Ver Wiel, took a perfectly sound story idea and complicated it into an exercise in style. Less is more.'

Chapter 13

A Career in Renaissance

No sooner was his work completed on W*ho Is Cletis Tout?*, in July 2001, than Christian was starting work on yet another movie the following month. Joining Nicolas Cage, he headed out to Hawaii to shoot *Windtalkers*, John Woo's World War II epic based on the true story of a group of Navajo Indians who used their ancient language as a military code that the Japanese were never able to crack. It was these code-talkers who helped the US to defeat the Japanese in the battles of Saipan and Iwo Jima in the South Pacific during the 1940s.

Although for this project Woo claims that he toned down the high carnage quotient that's such a familiar part of his movies – especially the ones he made in Hong Kong, such as *The Killer* and *Hard Target* – his sound team reckoned it was they who toned down the noise of the battlefield sequences. Woo fans needn't have worried, though; there were still plenty of battle scenes to satisfy. Even though Woo was cutting down on his usual diet of violence, the film still appealed to the director. 'It's a movie about friendship, patriotism and honour,' he said during the film's production. 'It's a very serious movie. Drama and action. *Real* action, you know? Not that kung-fu type. I intend to make the movie look very real and touching.'

Instead of the typical Woo shoot 'em up, *Windtalkers* focused on the relationship between Nicolas Cage's character – a US Marine who has been assigned to protect the Indian encryption expert – and one of the Navajos. As Joe Enders, Cage is a Marine sergeant who has been shattered, both physically and psychologically, by war. Enders develops a friendship with Private Carl Yahzee (played by Canadian actor Adam Beach), even though he has deadly orders to carry out if all goes wrong. His job is to prevent his young charge's capture from the Japanese at all cost – even if that means killing the encoder himself.

Yahzee and Enders are part of a reconnaissance unit whose orders are to move ahead of the larger Marine battalion and assess enemy positions, helping to target artillery fire and guide the direction of troops. Yahzee uses the code to relay co-ordinates by radio to Roger Willie's character, Whitehorse, a fellow code-talker who has also been assigned a guard, Ox, played by Christian.

Describing his character as big-hearted and charming, Christian, like Cage, was intrigued by Ox's conflict over his assignment as a guard. 'Enders has given up on human existence to some extent and seems more resigned to the assignment, but Ox really questions his orders.'

As one of the film's co-producers, Alison Rosenzweig, pointed out, 'Christian is a wonderful actor and audiences really respond to him. You're immediately drawn to his character. To see this likable person faced with such a devastating dilemma really packs an emotional punch.'

Like Cage, Christian was thrilled to be working with Woo again after their initial professional meeting on the set of *Broken Arrow*. Not only that but Christian was equally excited to explore new ground, having never been in a war film. 'It was an opportunity to pay tribute to the Marines and the Navajos, as well as to the time period and the war,' he enthused, 'and the opportunity to be a part of a story that was shedding light on a particular culture and a chapter in history that I didn't know anything about, so as I turned the pages it was really a history lesson for me. I had no idea the influence the Navajo Indians had in helping us to win the war and turn the tide. And of course, working with John Woo and Nick Cage really inspired me, as did playing this character – who's certainly a lot darker and a lot more war-weary [than anything else I've played]. This guy still had his heart. He was still connected to himself and willing to develop a friendship with a guy he had to protect.'

Christian also proved an invaluable ally to first-time actor Roger Willie, who relied heavily on Christian's experience. 'I would follow Christian,' Willie recalled. 'I trusted him and let him lead the way.' Willie had been selected from thousands of Navajos at an open casting call near his home in Colorado, which he had attended only in order to accompany his nephew, who was auditioning, so it's easy to imagine how thrilled he was to be cast in the role. 'There's a special quality to Roger,' confirmed producer Terence Chang. 'He has such a strong presence, such wisdom and intelligence.'

The story of the code-talkers is sacred to Willie, and it was an honour for him to portray one of his tribe's fabled heroes. 'It means a lot to me. I always viewed the code-talkers as special people. They are our own heroes.' Indeed, the code-talkers are treated with reverence in the Navajo community, and, as Willie said, 'The movie presents an opportunity for them and the Navajo people in general to be exposed to the entire world.'

It had taken literally years to develop the story of the code-talkers sufficiently for it to become a movie. Originally, co-producer Rosenzweig had seen the story of the Navajo's role in the war as a documentary, but her brother kept trying to persuade her that it would make a terrific big-screen adaptation. It was only when she discovered that each Navajo had a white bodyguard with orders to kill the man he was protecting if capture appeared imminent that she saw its potential as a movie. 'The moment I read that,' she recalled, 'I knew this could be a feature film.'

However, screenwriter John Rice, married to Rosenzweig's co-producing partner Tracie Graham, was not enthusiastic about the film at first: 'I thought it was a hard sell, even though I loved the moral dilemma from the get-go.'

The major obstacle was that of audience appeal. With Hollywood at that time releasing a large number of World War II films that featured Native Americans in lead roles, Rice was concerned. 'Could we have come up with any more strikes against us?' he lamented. After thirteen drafts, however, the screenplay came together, although there were still plenty of hurdles to overcome. 'I liked the idea of having a war as a background for red-man/white-man issues,' remembered Rice, 'and the more I thought about the more intrigued I became.'

Certainly, Rosenzweig felt that her passion for the project was fuelled by the theme and the characters, stating that the genre was far less important to her than the relationship between two men with diverse backgrounds: 'It's a story of their growing friendship – basically a heterosexual love story. Cage's character is psychologically wounded, emotionally unavailable, and he finds a new appreciation for life through Beach.'

After months of perfecting the movie pitch, the writers began to meet potential directors. 'We did every dramatic beat,' remembers Rice. 'It was a live staging. We became the characters, reciting twenty-five lines of the strongest dialogue.'

When Woo saw them run through the script, he loved the project. 'He stood up in the room and clapped and said, "That's my kind of movie,"' recalled Tracie Graham.

What perhaps made *Windtalkers* such a good movie was that it was based on a real-life situation. During the Second World War, scores of Navajo radio operators died at Saipan and Iwo Jima, even though there is no evidence of any being killed by the guards assigned to protect them. But the film nevertheless attracted some dissenting opinions; Sam Billison, who at the time of *Windtalkers'* release was the seventy-four-year-old president of the dwindling Navajo Code-Talkers Association, claimed that Hollywood was demoting the Native American's to a second role. He had spent a year in hospital, recovering from wounds he received in the conflict.

The Navajo language is one of the most complex in the world, with four tones, glottalised consonants, a click like that used in the South African Xhosa tribe's tongue and a thirty-five-letter alphabet. At the time of the Second World War, fewer than 80,000 people spoke Navajo, so it was an ideal language for transmitting sensitive information. Many of the 450 code-talkers were just out of school, but even the teenagers weren't spared the potential death penalty if they faced capture.

Although Nicolas Cage might have worked hard to get into shape for his character, he ducked out of going to a special boot camp that the other actors – including Christian – had to endure in order to get into shape for their roles. The course included a week of intensive training that Christian remembers was kind of scary. 'The first couple of days, we weren't really sure how seriously these drill sergeants were going to be taking their jobs, but they yelled in our faces and humiliated us and degraded us. When we first got there, they threw our duffel bags at us, and we all had to strip in a circle.'

The boot camp was something of a shock to the young star's system. 'Windtalkers opened my eyes to going through the boot-camp experience. It opened my eyes to more physical stuff that I was capable of doing, because the things that they asked us to do really forced us to dig deep into our souls. It's not like they lightened up on us. The beach marches we did and things like that just seemed to go on for miles and miles and miles. There were guys dropping out, gasping and wheezing for air.' Christian however kept going. 'Something in you says, "No, I cannot drop it." There's always some inner voice that keeps you trudging along.'

Despite the early-morning calls and long days of filming, perhaps it was the thought of being back on Hawaiian sand that kept Christian going. After all, what could be better than to return to Waikiki beach, where he and Ryan had reportedly spent most of their honeymoon and just one of the many locations around the exotic islands where Elvis Presley had made *Blue Hawaii* – one of Christian's favourite Elvis movies.

Windtalkers was released in America in June 2002 to general critical disdain. Roger Ebert was one of those who didn't particularly like it, writing in his review, 'The moment you decide to make *Windtalkers* a big-budget action movie with a major star and lots of explosions, flying bodies and stunt men, you give up any possibility that it can succeed on a human scale. The Navajo code-talkers have waited a long time to have their story told. Too bad it appears here merely as a gimmick in an action picture.'

Peter Travers, writing in *Rolling Stone*, agreed. 'However well staged, the limb-ripping carnage at the 1944 battle of Saipan feels generic compared to the racial and cultural battles that go begging. The code-talkers deserved better than a hollow tribute.'

And the review in the *San Francisco Chronicle* was even less complimentary: 'The best the movie can manage are some sweet interludes in which Ox (Slater) and his code-talker try to collaborate musically, trading phrases on the harmonica and Navajo flute and finding their way toward harmony. It's all very nice, but it leaves Enders out of the picture, and he *is* the picture – all scowling, enigmatic and empty.'

Long before the reviews rolled in, or indeed any preview

screenings had been seen, MGM decided that, to celebrate the film's release, they would hold a ceremony honouring the World War II Marine heroes that were depicted in the movie, followed by a reception (although strangely the film wasn't released until almost a year after the ceremony had been held, in Santa Monica in July 2001). At the ceremony, members of the United States Congress bestowed the Congressional Gold Medal – one of its highest honours – on the twenty-nine Navajo code-talkers who developed the code, while President George W Bush presented medals to four of the five living Navajo code-creators and the families of the others. Following the medal ceremony, the reception celebrated the honourees and heralded *Windtalkers*. After the ceremony that evening, a live report was broadcast via satellite that included a ninety-second edited news wrap-up and backstage shots of the ceremony, along with a clip of *Windtalkers* code-talkers in action and behind-the-scenes footage of the film.

The press release for the ceremony both applauded the film's story and, indeed, explained what it was truly about: 'In 1942, the twenty-nine Navajo Marines who are being honoured were sent as recruits to boot camp at the Marine Recruit Depot in San Diego, California. After boot camp, they were sent to Camp Elliot (modern-day Marine Corps Air Station Miramar) to develop a military code based on the Navajo language. Because Navajo is an unwritten language and has such a complex structure, it was a perfect choice upon which to base a secret code. Eventually around four hundred Navajo men were trained in the code's use and served as code-talkers in the Pacific battles of the war. The

Japanese were never able to break the code, and it became an indispensable tool for World War II military communication. Because of its success and its possible use in future combat, the code wasn't declassified until 1968, and the code-talkers' accomplishments went largely unheralded. The Congressional Gold Medal is the highest civilian honour that Congress can award. The first Gold Medal recipient was President George Washington. Other recipients include Thomas Edison, Rosa Parks, Bob Hope, Colin Powell, Gerald Ford, Norman Schwarzkopf and Mother Teresa of Calcutta.'

It was an historic occasion, one that recognised the heroic deeds of a people whose actions had long been forgotten since the end of the Second World War. And then, two months later, another war – the war on terror – took its first American victims.

On 11 September 2001, two planes flew into the World Trade Center buildings in New York and another hit the Pentagon in Washington, leaving untold numbers injured or dead and throwing both cities – and, indeed, the entire country – into chaos. As Christian told journalist Scott Lyle Cohen at the time, the reaction in California to the atrocities was no different to anywhere else in the country. 'There is definitely a sombre vibe. People are feeling devastated and shocked.' He could only imagine how people in New York must have been feeling while trying to regain some sense of normality within days of what had happened.

The tragedy had begun at the height of a morning rush hour in North America's largest city when a hijacked American Airlines jet slammed into one tower of the 110-

storey World Trade Center building. As smoke and flames poured out of the building and rescue workers battled to save victims, a second plane hit the adjacent tower. The two towers soon collapsed. Huge clouds of smoke hung over Manhattan. The nearby Wall Street financial markets were shut down. And then, a short time later, another plane struck the Pentagon, touching off a massive explosion and tearing a hole in one side of the building.

Six months before the tragedy, Christian had been promoting his next film, *Run for the Money*, or *Hard Cash*, as it was also known. In fact, the movie did little for his career in the lead-up to the financial devastation that 9/11 would have on world industry, including film-making. Although *Run for the Money* was originally intended for release in theatres, it ended up with only a television premiere and then headed straight to video stores' bottom shelves. To many reviewers, it was an indication of just how unforgiving Hollywood can be to its stars, specifically Christian and Val Kilmer, who had both somewhat fallen from grace at that time. And, to make matters worse, it was judged by most to be nothing more than a low-brow action-comedy with some added Tarantino-style dialogue for good effect.

However, there were some critics who didn't believe it was so bad it warranted a straight-to-video release. One of Christian's least-seen films, *Run for the Money* is, as the title hints, a movie that features a variety of cons and counter-cons as Christian's hustler and his band of bumbling buddies try to get a little bankroll for his child and girlfriend while trying to evade his greedy henchmen as well as a corrupt

FBI agent, played by Val Kilmer, Christian's old 'Elvis' ally from *True Romance*.

After *Run for the Money*, it was almost a year before the cinemagoing public saw Christian again on the big screen, and even then it was in another minor supporting role, this time as a roadie to Bob Dylan's character, Jack Tate, in *Masked and Anonymous*. According to the review in the *San Francisco Chronicle* and those in most other publications, *Masked and Anonymous* was 'a messy, ambitious comedy from writer Larry Charles, who spins out an apocalyptic yarn in which Jack, rock legend and son of a dying dictator, is sprung from jail to perform at a benefit concert'. As film critic Mike LaSalle pointed out, having Bob Dylan play the musical numbers was fine, and undoubtedly the best thing in the movie, but 'the dialogue scenes were disastrous. Void of inflection, Dylan doesn't act but stands and looks uneasy in whatever space the camera is pointing. The deadness in his eyes stops the movie cold.'

Cold or not, Larry Charles gathered an impressive supporting cast, most of whom worked below their level. John Goodman, for instance, played Uncle Sweetheart, a blustering yahoo who once managed Jack; Jessica Lange was a sleazy, lacquered concert promoter; and Jeff Bridges played a snoopy reporter hounding Jack. In fact, there's barely a speaking part that isn't played by a familiar name: in the movie, Penelope Cruz is Bridges's girlfriend, Angela Bassett a hooker, Val Kilmer a snake handler, Sean Penn and Christian are both roadies, and Mickey Rourke, Luke Wilson, Giovanni Ribisi and Cheech Marin also put in appearances.

Such an array of talent wasn't enough to save the movie

from the reviewers, including the *Chicago-Sun Times*'s Roger Ebert, who branded it 'a vanity production beyond all reason. I am not sure, however, that the vanity is Dylan's. I don't have any idea what to think about him. He has so long since disappeared into his persona that there is little received sense of the person there. The vanity belongs perhaps to those who flattered their own by working with him, by assuming (in the face of all they had learned during hard days of honest labour on a multitude of pictures) that his genius would somehow redeem a screenplay that could never have seemed other than what it was: incoherent raving juvenile meanderings.'

Larry Charles, however, expressed (in a somewhat grandiose fashion) his belief that the film was 'like the interior landscape of a great Bob Dylan song: rich with vivid imagery, poetic language and the dance of reality and illusion. For me, the movie has three fundamental themes. First, it is Bob Dylan on the road; second, it is about the social masks and armours we all wear to remain hidden and protected from one another; and third, it explores the role that destiny, fate and random circumstance play in our lives. It is an experimentation and exploration of the phenomenon of language itself.'

If *Masked and Anonymous* was a letdown, both critically and commercially, Christian's next few movies would fall into the same category. *Mindhunters* was especially curious, a film directed by Renny Harlin that had been lying in limbo for more than two years while at least three aborted release dates passed it by. It eventually made it on to American screens as late as May 2005, although it's perhaps surprising that it even made it into theatres at all.

As Roger Ebert noted, *Mindhunters* used what must be one of the most ancient and dependable formulas in the murder and thriller genre: that of attempting to surprise viewers with the killer's identity after arranging the evidence to point out one suspect after another until they persuasively clear their names by getting murdered. Indeed, to many reviewers, the plot of *Mindhunters* was altogether too much in the Agatha Christie style. Of course, in such films, characters routinely drive viewers to distraction by tempting fate – rushing off alone, for instance, or venturing into darkened rooms. Still, a few of the attacks depicted in *Mindhunters* had an elaborate, demented imagination behind them. And, at a time when too many characters smoke in movies, it was amusing to see at least one character die because she simply has to have a cigarette.

In *Mindhunters*, the suspects and victims are assembled on an isolated island that has been rigged up by the FBI as a training facility. It looks like a real town but is equipped with video cameras and hidden technology enabling supervisors to see how well trainees handle real-life problems (not that getting one's head shattered into super-cooled fragments is a challenge most FBI agents face every day on the job). Certainly, the formula was used early and well by Agatha Christie, whose influence on *Mindhunters* has been cited by such authorities as the *Hollywood Reporter* and *Film Threat*. In *The Mousetrap* – which has been running continuously in London's West End for over fifty years – she assembled a group of characters in a snowbound country house. One of them has died and the others try to solve the murder during long conversations in the sitting room involving much malt whiskey, considerable tobacco, unwise looks around the house and the revelation that some of the people are not really strangers to one another. It is possibly this play that gave us the phrase 'Where were you when the lights went out?'

As well as the Christie influence, Roger Ebert also noted that '*Mindhunters* adds another literary inspiration: George Orwell's "The Decline of the English Murder", a brilliant essay in which he celebrated the golden age of British poisoning and other ingenious methods of disposal. The victims were usually married to their killer, who tended to be a meek accountant who had fallen into a trap set by a floozy: "In the last analysis," Orwell writes, "he [commits] murder because this seems to him less disgraceful, and less damaging to his career, than being detected in adultery." But by 1946, when Orwell was writing, British standards had fallen off fearfully, and in the famous *Case of the Cleft-Chin Murder*, "The background was not domesticity, but the anonymous life of the dance-halls and the false values of the American film." So there we go again, vulgar Americans with our wicked influence on the Brits, who in murder as elsewhere maintained elegant traditions until we spoiled the game by just having people kill each other.

'Orwell might have been cheered by *Mindhunters*, although Christie would have wanted a more ingenious solution. They both might have thought that the killer in the movie goes to a dubious deal of difficulty to create elaborate murder situations that depend on perfect timing, skilful mechanics, a deep knowledge of the characters and a single-minded focus on providing the movie with "gotcha!" scenes.

Does the killer in any one of these movies ever have a moment of weariness and depression?'

Not in *Mindhunters*, they don't, concluded Ebert: 'The people who arrive on the island are there for an exercise in the profiling of a mass killer. Can they construct a psychological profile to narrow the search to the likely suspects? Val Kilmer plays their instructor, as the kind of expert you suspect has studied *The Dummies' Guide to Profiling*. The others include LL Cool J as Gabe Jensen, a Philadelphia cop who is along as an observer; the brainy Sara Moore (Kathryn Morris); the sexy Nicole Willis (Patricia Velasquez); Vince Sherman (Clifton Collins Jr), who uses a wheelchair; JD Reston (Christian Slater) as a cocky showboat, and so on.

'They all have a single character trait, announced with such frequency that apparently, when they packed for the island, they were allowed to bring along only one. There is the character who likes to smoke. The character who will not go anywhere without a gun. Perhaps not amazingly, each victim dies because of the weakness revealed by his trait. The ingenuity of their deaths is impressive. Murder traps are rigged all over the island. You may think they are unbelievably complicated, but I say they're nothing a rogue agent couldn't accomplish if he was assisted by an army of key grips, carpenters, best boys, electricians, set designers, art directors, special-effects wizards, make-up experts and half a dozen honey wagons.

'Is the film worth seeing? Well, yes and no. Yes, because it is exactly what it is, and no, for the same reason. What always amuses me ... is how the survivors keep right on talking, scheming, suspecting and accusing. They persist while bodies are piling up like cordwood. At some point, even if you were FBI material, wouldn't you run around screaming and looking for a boat so you could row the hell off that island?

'The mystery, when it is solved, is both arbitrary and explained at great length. The killer gives a speech justifying his or her actions, which is scant comfort for those already dead. As a courtesy, why not post a notice at the beginning: "The author of a series of murders that will begin this evening would like his victims to know in advance that he has good reasons, which follow."'

Of course, expert profilers might be able to read such a note and figure out the killer's identity – although not, many suspected, in this movie. As Ebert correctly suggested, 'If you have never seen *The Third Man*, I urge you to rent it immediately, as a preparation (or substitute) for *Mindhunters*.' Elsewhere, the movie was deemed as being of 'a slightly grungy, B-movie style that satisfies the subject matter while doing nothing to elevate it. The performances, too, are adequate but unexceptional.'

Chapter 14

So Be It

Christian's next movie, *Churchill: The Hollywood Years*, also turned out to be something of a curiosity. To this day, it still awaits release in America, and even in Britain, where it was set to become the Christmas blockbuster of 2004 while Christian entered the third month of his London run in *One Flew Over the Cuckoo's Nest*, the film ended up with a limited release, disappointing box office and bad reviews. In fact, most critics found the whole concept preposterous from the outset, and some even thought the film-makers would have been better off if they had abandoned the script altogether and simply filmed the making of it, releasing instead footage of the goings-on behind the scenes. According to one online reviewer, the film was nothing more than 'a heavy-going spoof with one joke that's stretched to snapping point, and should have been a sketch on late-night TV. It's a deliberately crass, blockbuster-style take on our illustrious wartime Prime

Minister, with the studio deciding the real Winston was "too fat, too old and too English". So we get Christian Slater as Churchill the Marine, triumphing over *'Allo 'Allo* Nazis and wooing Queen Elizabeth (a game Neve Campbell). Simply a bad movie.'

Churchill: The Hollywood Years told the story of American GI Winston Churchill, who has returned to London to drum up support for the war against Hitler's Third Reich. Back in the UK, reigning monarch King George has no time to consider the foibles of a war with the Germans. Even the efforts of his servant, Lord W'ruff, who surreptitiously places a copy of *Mein Kampf* by his bed, fail to draw the King's attention to the raging war in Europe. Besides, he has two daughters to keep his eye on: Elizabeth, a caring and diligent young princess, and Margaret, an unruly party animal intent on having a good time and little else. Spurred on by the suffering in war-torn Europe, Elizabeth feels that she must contribute to the war effort, while Margaret couldn't care less and mocks Elizabeth's desire to help the common man, an attitude that serves only to strengthen Elizabeth's conviction. Enlisting as 'Jane Commoner', the UK's future Queen reports for duty at the local military drafting centre.

Having arrived in London, Winston Churchill and his compatriot Dwight D Eisenhower head straight to Military High Command, where, unbeknownst to them, young Princess Elizabeth has been stationed. Churchill presents Lord W'ruff with the German Enigma machine – the key to cracking encoded German radio transmissions – and at the same time suggests that they use the machine to feed the Germans false intelligence by broadcasting bogus radio orders commanding an invasion of southern France, then pile into Normandy and catch the Gerries with their pants down.

W'ruff isn't interested. He's way too busy sipping a cup of tea and nibbling on a rock cake. Placating Churchill with feigned thanks for this lovely gift, he charges one of his commanders, Baxter, with the task of showing Churchill the proverbial door. Young Princess Elizabeth, however, is moved by Churchill's passion and drive to fight the good fight and she follows Churchill outside, tells him that he is appreciated and that he must never give up, as her country needs him.

Churchill is somewhat taken with the beautiful Elizabeth and persuades her to come down the East End for a pint or two with Jim Charoo and the 'Irish cockneys'. Charoo succeeds in cajoling Elizabeth to dance a jig with Churchill, but she can't dance and ends up in an embarrassing heap on the floor. Both physically and mentally bruised by the incident, Elizabeth flees. Churchill dashes after her but, despite his attempts to console the Princess, Elizabeth dashes off.

Lord W'ruff awaits a clandestine visitor flying in at Heathrow Airport (which didn't even exist during the Second World War — an apparently unintentional anachronism). On landing, the plane disgorges his guests: the Fuehrer himself, Adolf Hitler; his lady friend, Eva Braun; and his bodyguards, Roberts and Bormann, in tow. W'ruff endeavours to get Hitler and his entourage into London, but he hadn't counted on his car breaking down. The party manage to jump-start the car, but Hitler, sitting in the driving seat, loses control of the vehicle and crashes into a wall.

On quitting the car, W'ruff leads the group to the nearest road so that they can hitch a ride into London. They succeed in securing the services of a local taxi, but the driver mistakes the Fuehrer for Charlie Chaplin, congratulates Adolf on his star turn in *The Gold Rush* and ends up lying dead in a burning taxi. W'ruff is then forced to make alternative plans and the party boards a bus, only to find that their conductor cannot take them to their location, as it's not on his route. Following his summary execution, and with the bus under their control, W'ruff and Hitler make haste to their final destination: Buckingham Palace.

Churchill, meanwhile, discovers that he is to be deported at the orders of Lord W'ruff himself, and Baxter is only too happy to see that the orders are carried out. However, a surprise personal invitation to Buckingham Palace from King George grants Churchill a reprieve, much to Baxter's anger. When Churchill arrives at the palace, however, he discovers that he has been invited to celebrate the birthday of Princess Elizabeth and not to discuss the war in Europe with King George. The King is too concerned about the cost of the birthday bash and is monitoring his guests to make sure they don't indulge too heartily on his money.

Churchill greets Prince Elizabeth, at which point he discovers that it was she who invited him and not her father. They confess that they've both been dreaming about each other and escape to a secret room as the party starts to wind down.

Meanwhile, Hitler has arrived at the palace with W'ruff, Eva and his pet dog, Waffles. The Fuehrer dotes on his canine friend, while W'ruff and the palace courtiers, Potter and Bendle, pounce upon Elizabeth and Churchill as they reacquaint themselves in the secret room. They take Elizabeth to her quarters and Churchill is sent to be dealt with by Baxter.

Later, Churchill and Eisenhower are set free by Baxter out in the countryside, only to be hunted down like game by Baxter's soldiers. However, the two Americans succeed in disarming Baxter and, each toting a machine gun, rush to the airport to hijack a plane back to America. But Churchill is injured by a well-placed shot from one of Baxter's men and is forced to remain while Eisenhower wings it back to Washington. He manages to evade his captors, escaping to the quaint little village of Frothington-on-the-Waddle, where he calls Elizabeth, and together they vow to put a stop to the Germans. Elizabeth takes the underground Royal Train direct from Buckingham Palace to meet with Churchill at a remote train-station café, reminiscent of the one in Noël Coward's *Brief Encounter*.

Later still, Churchill and Elizabeth meet up with loyal friend Jim Charoo as they plan the defeat of Hitler, when suddenly they are attacked by a group of Germans. Charoo is slain, but Churchill and Elizabeth escape on the Royal Train and head back to London for a final confrontation with the Fuehrer.

On the train, Churchill and Elizabeth dine in luxury, being waited on hand and foot by Elizabeth's personal servant, Chester. They spend the night together in transit, locked in tight embrace, but the next morning a German patrol storms the train, capturing Elizabeth and leaving

Churchill and Chester to continue their journey to Buckingham Palace by themselves.

Back at the Palace, Hitler tells an imprisoned Elizabeth of his plan to marry her that very day. Distraught at her lover's rejection, Eva leaves Hitler, taking his precious Waffles with her, while Hitler is groomed for his big day. Churchill arrives and confronts Hitler, but he is overpowered and imprisoned by the Fuehrer's henchmen. All seems lost until Eva decides to wreak revenge on Hitler and frees Churchill from his shackles so that he can stop the marriage ceremony. He interrupts the ceremony just as the final vows are being exchanged, saving Elizabeth and prompting Hitler to flee with the Princess's sister, Margaret, deciding that, if he can't have one sister, he'll take the other. Eisenhower arrives, bringing the US cavalry with him, and they all chase Hitler. Nevertheless, the Fuehrer escapes to fight another day.

Churchill then returns to the frontline to fight against the Third Reich, and at the close of the war he returns to Buckingham Palace to receive his knighthood from the newly crowned Queen Elizabeth. They know that they shouldn't, that she's a Queen and he's only an American, that these things just shouldn't happen and must remain forever unrequited, but that just wouldn't be right, so they confess their undying love for each other, consummating their love with a long and passionate kiss.

On its release, *Churchill: The Hollywood Years* came in for some rough treatment from the critics, including *The Times*'s Wendy Ide, who reported to her readers, 'The humour was largely underpants-based and of the all-mincing, all-flouncing gay stereotype variety, which probably keeps the sniggering pre-pubescent schoolboy contingent happy. It looked like a barefaced insult to the rest of the audience.'

If there was any saving grace for the film, it was the stellar cast of British comedy that was assembled. Indeed, *Churchill: The Hollywood Years* was possibly the first British movie since the heyday of the *Carry On* franchise to feature a host of establishment talent, such as Leslie Phillips, Rik Mayall and Harry Enfield, sharing the screen with relative newcomers from the small screen's *The League of Gentlemen*, *The Office* and *Smack the Pony*, including McKenzie Crook, Steve Pemberton, Sally Phillips and James Dreyfus.

Even if the critics didn't like the film that much, perhaps what should be considered is how cinema has always had a strange relationship with the truth. Back in 1934, a major Hollywood studio was successfully sued over a biopic of the mad monk Rasputin that claimed – wrongly, as it turned out – the debauched 'spiritual adviser' had seduced a clearly recognisable member of the Russian royal family. The consequences were swift, and concerns of similar pitfalls remain with film-makers to this day.

Indeed, anyone who has sat through a film claiming to be based on a true story, in which the names of the protagonists have been retained, might be puzzled to see the same disclaimer time after time: 'The events and characters depicted in this photo play are fictitious. Any similarity to actual persons, living or dead, is purely coincidental.' But what began as a mere safety measure to protect against libel suits has allowed Hollywood to play fast and loose with the facts of history.

In recent years, cinemagoers have been surprised to see

films depicting Americans liberating the Enigma machine from the Nazis, the defence of Stalingrad being led by a sex symbol apparently straight from London's Primrose Hill and the SS *Titanic* going down with works of art that are still very much available to view in galleries around the world. One such movie, dealing with the behaviour of the British army during the American Civil War, was summarily dismissed by a leading authority on the subject, who claimed that it was to history what '*Godzilla* was to biology'.

The writer and director of *Churchill: The Hollywood Years*, Peter Richardson, perhaps pre-empted this trend in February 1988 with the airing of his hour-long TV comedy *The Strike* (shown as part of the influential *Comic Strip* series of films), in which a naïve writer hears that his account of the 1984 miners' strike is to become a major motion picture. Before his eyes, his well-meaning work of art becomes an out-of-control juggernaut, much in the style of Hugh Hudson's troubled epic *Revolution*, starring Al Pacino.

The theme of celebrity has recurred on numerous occasions in Richardson's work, chiefly in his satire *Stella Street*, a UK comedy series in which an unlikely pack of actors and rock stars (played mostly by Phil Cornwell and John Sessions) move into a suburban cul de sac. But in *Churchill: The Hollywood Years*, Richardson made his most adventurous assault on the subject yet, with real Hollywood stars deconstructing a crucial moment in British history. At the whim of a desperate, low-rent producer, the legendary British Prime Minister Winston Churchill is transformed from a jowly, bald curmudgeon into a dashing GI who becomes romantically involved with the future Queen of

England while trying to foil a takeover bid masterminded by the traitorous Lord W'ruff on behalf of Adolf Hitler.

As producer Jonathan Cavendish explains, 'Peter had been developing the script for quite some time, and he'd had the idea of making a film that was, at the centre of the piece, a spoof of the American way of rewriting and re-devising history. And I was very taken with that idea too, having seen a lot of those types of movies. From *Pearl Harbor* to *U-571*, everything seems to be seen only from the American point of view. Now, they make them very well, and commercially they're a sound idea, but we thought it would be interesting to make a film that poked a little bit of fun at that. Although I must say that both Peter and I are huge fans of American movies; I bet that, if we both came up with our top-ten lists of movies, eight of them would be American, and like all the best satire, [*Churchill: The Hollywood Years*] is affectionate. We're not satirising anything other than the editorial attitude of some American studios in the present day.'

From that simple starting point, Richardson and writer Peter Richens – with input from Cavendish and the likes of Harry Enfield, Rik Mayall and John Sessions, among others – felt that they had crafted a surreal romp that threw all the basic tenets of history out of the window. Timescales shift and fuse but become seductively plausible, until the whole film seems to take place in a parallel dimension in which Buckingham Palace houses its own underground station, the Royal Train is a high-velocity getaway vehicle and Adolf Hitler owns a dog named Waffles. As Cavendish puts it, 'We turn it all inside out and upside down and all around the place. The film is really what happens logically, or perhaps illogically, when the first thing you do is make the leading character in your story – i.e. Winston Churchill – an American instead of an Englishman, because you've discovered that Churchill was in fact a large, balding, middle-aged man who is not going to sell the film in Kansas. And so you've cast the film using the guy who was just in an action-adventure thriller. Once you've done that, you have an absolute licence to run with that.'

The first step was to select who would play the lead, as this would set the whole tone for the production. 'Once you hear the title,' revealed Cavendish, 'you get the gist of where it's going.' By casting Christian, at the age of thirty-four some thirty years younger than the real Churchill, Richardson and co were sure that this would signal their intentions. And, as Christian pointed out, 'I guess there's not much funny about World War Two, but there have been so many war movies based on that time period lately. I was in one, *Windtalkers*, and so it seems they've really covered every angle of World War Two. They've really paid homage to that time period and it's been taken very seriously, so it just feels right to make a comedy about these types of movies. It pokes fun at Hollywood, American patriotism and the English aristocracy, which is a nice blend. It makes fun of both sides and has a really good time doing it.'

Costume designer James Keast agreed with Christian: 'When I read the script, I thought, This is actually a fantastic opportunity to ignore the period, because it's not actually set in the real 1940s or even the 1930s, so you've got the freedom to do what you like. Princess Elizabeth and her sister, Princess Margaret, were only six and eight around that time, but in our script they're sixteen and eighteen. Most of the images you see when they're of that age are from the 1950s, so in our film most of the clothes they're wearing are 1950s rather than proper period Second World War. My attitude going into it was, don't let the period get in the way of telling the story. It's a comedy, so, if what I've done isn't correct to the period, it doesn't matter, as long as it tells a story. That's why we have Princess Margaret looking 1950s and have the East Enders looking like something from *Oliver* rather than the 1940s.'

Having parodied the concept of movie stars in both *The Strike* and *Stella Street*, Richardson knew that the success of *Churchill: The Hollywood Years* depended on real star power. As Cavendish continued, 'We knew that our biggest danger was being seen to be televisual rather than filmic, and I think that's why Peter came to me, as someone who'd made big and small comic films. The technical personnel on the movie are all major movie people, the casting is filmic and the locations are big and grand. It's a proper movie in every conceivable way.'

This was also the reason why they decided to enlist top-drawer, big-name talent to play the lead role. Christian was their first choice, and recruiting him – and others in the cast – turned out to be a much easier pitch than they had expected. 'It was very interesting when we went to America for the casting,' recalled Cavendish, 'because there was an unbelievably powerful response from the agents and the actors. Everyone seemed to want to be in it. First of all, it was a very funny script, and Peter's reputation in America is there – people have heard of him and want to work with him – but also it seemed that a lot of people in America are very open to this sort of satire.'

Certainly, by his own admission, Christian didn't take a lot of persuading to take on a role that required him to up-end his action-hero image. 'I read the script and, to be honest, I wasn't quite sure what to make of it at first, but I had a meeting with Peter, we sat down and talked and had a good chuckle about it. I wasn't exactly sure which direction it was going to go in. It was kind of described to me as a Monty Python-ish type comedy, and I like Monty Python a lot, but it was kind of hard to get a general sense of things. But after being on the set for just a couple of days, and seeing a lot of the slapstick insanity and guys like Vic Reeves and Bob Mortimer doing crazy stuff and ad-libbing, I knew pretty much from day one the kind of movie that it was – just wacky, quirky, zany fun.'

Having seen the machinations of Hollywood first-hand, Christian was quick to appreciate the irony. 'The real Winston Churchill was incredibly historic, but he wasn't really good at wielding a machine gun, so I guess someone decided to "youthen" him up a little. Hollywood movies always have to cast a hero as a hero, and heroes can't be fat men in their sixties with no hair and treble chins. And they can't be British, either, because that just wouldn't work for them. So I think that's where the comedy lies: if Americans get hold of a story and the hero isn't quite what they expect, then they'll adapt the hero to become what they want the hero to be.'

Once he knew what kind of character this movie Churchill had to be, Christian set about finding a role model, and his own action-movie history helped to prepare him for what was needed. 'A film like *Broken Arrow* is a very, very patriotic, gung-ho type of thing, but really, in a way, it was kind of a comic book. *Churchill: The Hollywood Years* has, for me, been a completely unique experience. I've never really done an outright comedy before, but it's pretty much the same thing: taking a real level of commitment and just going for it. Knowing what you want to do and who your character is, and then just letting yourself go.'

Rather than draw on his own experiences, Christian looked to the canon of classic action heroes. 'There are certain characteristics that Winston Churchill possessed that we did take, like his features and his cigar,' he affirmed. 'There are definitely some tributes there in the film to the great man that he was, but for the most part I did have to come up with some things for myself and basically just keep America in mind. I was studying other action films, other action stars, like Bruce Willis. My character is really representing America here. I'm the gung-ho epitome of the patriotic guy. I'm determined that we're going to win the war, but I keep bumping into these people, these crazy English people, who just don't seem to care, or even want a war. My character's saying, "Let's go! We're fighting! We've gotta fight the war! We've gotta win the war!" But they seem to have a more laid-back, casual attitude than I do.'

Cavendish agrees. 'Christian was playing Bruce Willis playing Churchill from the outset, and he was very clear about what he wanted to be doing from the get-go.'

Costume designer James Keast went out of his way in his tailoring to reflect this attitude. 'It's really Bruce Willis in *Die*

Hard. Winston's a GI in a vest, and that's the piss-take throughout the whole thing – except when he's dressed up for a party, and then the look becomes Richard Gere in *An Officer and a Gentleman.* If you watch *Die Hard,* you'll see that Bruce Willis's wardrobe chiefly consists of a vest and a shirt and various versions of that, which is exactly what we've done here.'

With Christian recruited, Richardson realised that his ambitious casting plans would be easier to realise than he had anticipated. When Antony Sher was asked to play Adolf Hitler in the film, his reaction was sanguine. 'That's just a delightful central joke to the film, that in Hollywood the war couldn't possibly have been won by that old English man smoking a cigar; he's got to be portrayed as a hunky GI. I think that's delightful. It appealed to me no end.'

Having found his Churchill and Hitler, Richardson was then faced with the challenge of finding an actress to play the love interest: the young Princess Elizabeth and future Queen of England. Again, it was decided that an established Hollywood star – in this case, Canadian-born Neve Campbell – would perhaps be well suited to the role. Neve played Princess Elizabeth more credibly than an English actress might have done, but also with a comic edge. Her accent, deportment and appearance are all uncannily believable, and she looks just like the young Princess Elizabeth did at that age.

It helped that both Christian and Neve are anglophiles. 'They've both spent time in England, they like the English sense of humour and, most crucially, they've got a very good sense of humour themselves,' insisted Cavendish.

Indeed, it was the humour that drew Campbell to the

script, despite her roots in more straight-faced movies such as the *Scream* trilogy. 'You read a lot of bad scripts,' she explains, 'but you very rarely pick up a good comedy. They're really hard to write. In the States, we tend to try to make these romantic comedies that are trying to be funny and trying to be meaningful at the same time, but they very rarely manage to do either of those. But with this kind of comedy, where it's just straight up and out there, I laughed throughout. It's the kind of British humour I grew up with in Canada. My dad really got me into it when I was a kid; I watched *Black Adder* and *Monty Python* and a lot of the TV shows here on the BBC, so I definitely got it.'

Neve is also aware that comedy is something that's really hard to do well. 'It's almost easier to do drama if you can get into a character and you can understand their emotion, and you're capable of doing it, but comedy is really specific: how to tell a joke; how to deliver a joke and have it be realistic and viable as well. It was a challenge, but I loved that challenge.'

Richardson was pleased to see how well Campbell's take on Elizabeth worked alongside Christian's Churchill, and the actress was equally impressed with her co-star. 'Christian's great,' she enthused. 'He's played the hero roles and he's been in the business so long, people see him as this one thing, but he's really good at comedy. He's really funny, it turns out. It seems corny – there are all the corny lines, all the corny characteristics of a hero in any film – except that we play it up so much, we're making fun of those films and that kind of character.'

Christian was equally thrilled to be working with Campbell. 'I was so impressed, honestly, with Neve's level of commitment,' he gushed. 'She's playing Princess Elizabeth as this doe-eyed, lost little innocent girl who's looking for an adventure. And Winston Churchill comes along and they kind of both sweep each other off their feet.'

While *Churchill: The Hollywood Years* might not have lived up to its promise, Christian's next movie, *Alone in the Dark*, was also something of a disappointment. Released in America at the beginning of 2005, but yet to surface as a theatrical release in Britain at the time of writing, the film was hated by critics. As the *San Francisco Examiner*'s Christy Lemire noted, it was a dark mess. 'As movies based on video games go, *Alone in the Dark* almost makes you long for the quaint days of *Tron*, or at least hope that something more sophisticated is on the horizon. *Pong: The Musical*, perhaps. For now, if we choose to accept it, we have this: a messy action flick that's an inept cross between the *Alien* movies and the *Indiana Jones* trilogy. But we shouldn't hate it on Tara Reid alone, who's described in the movie's production notes as "a brilliant anthropologist". And, although it's not even a comedy, she gets help in the unintentional hilarity department from Christian Slater, playing a paranormal investigator named Edward Carnby who also happens to be Reid's ex-boyfriend.

'Anyway, some evil experiments were conducted on a bunch of the kids with whom Edward grew up in an orphanage. Edward managed to escape. Twenty-two years later, all those kids have grown up and disappeared, but seem to have been turned into crude *Alien*-esque monsters.'

Another, even more condemning review tagged the film as 'by far the worst movie of 2005, hands down, and it's not even

February yet. All right, so Christian Slater has made some bad career choices in the past, but what on earth was he thinking, taking this role on? Director Uwe Boll messed up back in 2003 by trying to turn the video game *House of Dead* into a movie, and you would think he learned his lesson. Nope. He does it to himself again, trying to remake the old Atari game *Alone in the Dark* into a film. The movie follows the paranormal detective Edward Carnby, played by Slater, in his attempt to unravel the mysteries of his clouded past. This past of his isn't normal, either; oh no, it involves an orphanage, a crazy scientist and low-budget computer-animated demons.

'Even going into the movie expecting some mindless but cool entertainment didn't pan out for this one. After twenty or so minutes, you'll find yourself wondering if you can still catch the previews of the movie playing on the screen next door. The beginning is pretty cool. They set up a creative plot and get you pretty psyched about what's to come, demons and all, but then it just bombs.

'Even Tara Reid and Stephen Dorff were no match for the horridness of this flick. Reid, Dorff and Slater all seemed like they were reading their lines for the first time, and all the smaller background acting felt like watching a really bad sitcom, with enough unnatural movement and emotions to fill five phone booths.

'The moment when you really just put your face into your hands and start to weep is when Reid, out of absolutely nowhere, shows up at Slater's house and just climbs into bed with him. When a director can actually succeed at making Tara Reid getting into bed look bad, then you know it's time to leave.

'There needs to be some sort of organisation that puts an end to making video games into movies, and stops people like Uwe Boll and Paul WS Anderson from touching movie cameras ever again. If another *Alone in the Dark* or *Alien vs Predator* comes out again, heads are going to roll. Who knows what Slater was thinking but, if he wants to start making a name for himself again, he had better go back to his skateboarding days of *Gleaming the Cube* and *The Wizard.*'

With a UK release of *Alone in the Dark* still unannounced (perhaps unsurprisingly, considering the American reviews), and with a batch of other films – maybe just as bad – still awaiting release, Christian's most recent film projects seem to reflect some pretty poor choices. Even *The Deal*, which was premiered at the 2004 AFI Film Festival and is also still awaiting release, didn't sound all that promising either.

According to a synopsis of the completed film that appeared on the project's official internet site, the movie is set in a war in the Middle East during the worst oil shortage in US history. Gas prices skyrocket, further weakening an already faltering economy, and Wall Street is hobbled by corruption. The nation is on edge.

Against this chaos, Wall Street big shot Tom Hanson (Christian) is shocked to learn of the death of his best friend, Richard Kester (Paul McGillion), a top executive for one of the nation's leading oil companies, Condor. But, when he's approached by Richard's boss, Jared Tolsen (Robert Loggia), to advise on a big oil merger his friend was working on, he jumps at the chance to kickstart his faltering career.

At the same time, idealistic business-school graduate

Abbey Gallagher (Selma Blair) is convinced by Tom to join his prestigious investment bank to work on a deal that promotes alternative energy use. Tom finds himself unexpectedly drawn to Abbey's energy and enthusiasm – qualities long since lost in him. Sexual tension builds and they embark on a risky love affair.

Tom starts researching the Condor deal, setting up a merger with Russian oil company Black Star, and soon discovers that things are not as they should be. Black Star's oil regions are dry, yet they still manage to deliver scarce oil to the US. Digging deeper, Tom begins to uncover a global conspiracy of illegal oil trafficking, government cover-ups and murder.

Tom receives threats and is forced to distance himself from Abbey to protect her. Believing he might be involved in something illegal, Abbey begins her own investigation, which leads to her being kidnapped by the Russian Mafia when she too learns too much. With the clock ticking, Tom has to put his career, his reputation and even his life in jeopardy to protect Abbey and expose the truth about the deal.

The next film on Christian's release list was the equally unpromising (or so it seemed) *The Good Shepherd*. Premiered at the Cannes Film Festival in May 2004 and at Montreal in the same month that Christian would return to the stage in *One Flew Over the Cuckoo's Nest* at the Edinburgh Fringe Festival, the film was another yet to miss out on a theatrical release, and has so far appeared only as a cable-TV premiere or a straight-to-video release. Otherwise, it has been completely overlooked.

Chapter 15

Flung Out of the Cuckoo's Nest

In the winter of 2003, in Las Vegas, Christian ended up with a gash over his left ear, inflicted by his wife, Ryan Haddon. According to *People Weekly* magazine, on 10 November, at about 7am, Christian 'stumbled out of an elevator at the Hard Rock Hotel and Casino, bleeding and saying, "My wife's fucking crazy." While the actor, a guest at the luxe property, was quickly hustled outside by employees to await an ambulance, officers arrived and later arrested Haddon. A police source said Slater initially told cops his wife threw a glass at him during an argument, but then changed his story when told she would be arrested because of Nevada's strict laws regarding domestic-violence suspects. Slater's second account, which a source says he's sticking to, maintains that it was all an "accident", that he and Haddon were "joking around" and that the glass slipped from her hand. Slater, thirty-four, received nine stitches at the Desert Springs Hospital, while Haddon, thirty-two, was fingerprinted, photographed, booked on a misdemeanour battery/domestic-violence charge and, twelve hours later, released from the Clark County Detention Center.'

One month later, in December 2003, it was decided that Haddon wouldn't face criminal charges after all for injuring her husband. Clark County District Attorney David Roger said that there was no proof she intended to hurt Christian when she hit him with a drinking glass. 'We did not feel we could prove beyond a reasonable doubt that she committed intentional battery. Both the victim and the defendant maintained that it was an accident. Clearly there was no criminal wrongdoing.'

The alleged attack was considered by many to be the beginning of the end of what was perhaps an already troubled relationship, although many still considered it strange that only twelve months earlier Christian had won a lavish spread in *Hello!* magazine about 'the quiet life' he was now living at 'the stunning home he shared with his wife and children'. Given Christian's hellraising background, it certainly astounded the magazine that his home didn't reflect anything at all from his bad-boy past. If anything, his west Los Angeles house was a haven of cosy domesticity and, as far as the magazine was concerned, spoke volumes of his passion for gardening as one of his favourite pastimes.

'When the garden is in full swing,' reported Ryan in the *Hello!* feature, 'it looks like the south of France.' Indeed, the photo set depicted a riot of fruit trees and potted blooms lining sunbaked stone steps leading down to a garden, the couple's light, airy home boasting an abundance of windows and French doors opening on to an expanse thick with geraniums, herbs, jasmine, stephanotis and old-fashioned climbing roses. 'It's an outdoor house and the doors are open all summer long,' Ryan pointed out.

Inside the house, each room – living room, playroom, breakfast area, kitchen and small home office on the ground floor; three bedrooms and a family room on the first – has been lovingly decorated in natural shades and soft floral prints, reflecting the couple's love for their garden. To obtain the effect and create the right ambience, Ryan worked with leading Los Angeles designer Lynn von Kersting. 'I had some trepidation about using a decorator,' she confessed, 'but Lynn worked in a wonderful way. She gave me books to look at, took me shopping. I chose the materials I liked and she knew how each could best be used.' Ultimately, Ryan felt that the results were well worth the effort, with luxurious cotton chenille, old French silks and heavy textured linens combining to create a mood of harmony and romance.

Indeed, French influences are found throughout the house, echoing Ryan's childhood, which was spent largely in an upmarket quarter of Paris, but the house also reflected her later travels through Asia; in the living room, a nineteenth-century Indian mahogany bed works beautifully as a coffee table, displaying an assortment of books, a marble Buddha, colourful fruit arrangements from their garden and mementoes of their travels. A small, exquisite pagoda sits on a nearby chest while another Buddha decorates a mantel-piece. All around are beautifully framed and clearly treasured pictures of the couple and their family. As *Hello!* magazine's reporter Tommy Cohen pointed out, 'This successful meeting of East and West mirrors the unlikely but harmonious marriage of the house's owners – the former out-of-control jailbird actor and the sophisticated, career-minded TV executive. For Christian, who could have easily gone the same way as River Phoenix, it's a union that has turned his life around.'

At the time, Christian credited Ryan as being 'the person who has dispelled the bad-boy image that I had and the person who has brought me serenity'. He then revealed, 'I have built a foundation that works. We're learning how to be parents, developing ways that are right for us.'

Ryan agreed, even though she knew that they'd been very lucky. 'There is always the promise in life that we'll meet someone [special]. I knew Christian was different. Our pact was a spiritual one right from the start.'

It was, however, not to last. Just over one year later, in January 2005, Britain's *Mail on Sunday* reported that Ryan had thrown Christian out of their elegant rented house in London's Little Venice after a furious argument and threatened to take their children home to America. In the newspaper feature, reporters Angelina Johnson and Deborah Collcutt noted that it had been 'after midnight in a dimly lit private member's club in Soho that Christian, fresh from a performance of *One Flew Over the Cuckoo's Nest*, had been seen huddled in a corner with a glamorous brunette gazing into his eyes'. That, perhaps, was the problem.

Christian's representatives, of course, discreetly let it be known that the split was no more than a trial separation, but the 1,500-word *Mail on Sunday* article stated that the break-up was far more serious. 'The thorny issue at the heart of the row is said to be Slater's stubborn refusal to grow up and take seriously his responsibilities as a husband and father.' Indeed, only one month later, Christian filed for divorce.

When Christian arrived in Britain the previous summer to play Randle Patrick McMurphy in *One Flew Over the Cuckoo's Nest*, the producers knew that the play would provide an ideal opportunity for a West End debut and with a bankable Hollywood name in the lead role, how could they go wrong? It was a well-worn strategy used to great success by stars such as Nicole Kidman, Kim Cattrall and Kevin Spacey. For Christian, it also gave him a chance to revitalise a career that had until then been tarnished by some poor movie choices, drink, drugs and a couple of stints in prison and rehab.

When *The Sunday Times* caught up with him for a December 2004 feature, however, he was already thinking about why he wanted to join the growing list of American film stars seeking a better life in the United Kingdom. 'If I had to choose one of Britain's main national characteristics,' he mused, 'I guess it would be self-deprecation, particularly when it comes to talking about the country itself. But I have to say it really does seem one of the greatest places on Earth. I've been to Britain a few times before, but I hadn't really thought of moving here until five months ago, when I came to work on *One Flew Over the Cuckoo's Nest* in Edinburgh. Since starting the show, my family and I have become genuinely excited about the possibility of moving to Britain. We've even begun looking for a house, albeit haphazardly. We've fallen in love with the place.

'Before I arrived, I was warned about British reserve. American friends said people over here just weren't as gregarious as Americans tend to be. I was pleasantly surprised to find that not to be the case. People here have been warm, welcoming and enthusiastic. I haven't experienced any serious anti-American feeling. People discuss the war a lot, but it doesn't seem like they're opposed to Americans in general: perhaps just the current administration.

'One of the things that puts some actors off London is the paparazzi, but I've found those guys surprisingly protective. I was coming out of a restaurant recently with my wife, and one of them took me aside and told me to be careful – he pointed out a guy nearby on a motorbike and said that he'd heard he planned to follow us. That was a little creepy, and he was right. I still don't know if it was another paparazzi [*sic*] or an assassin, but I'm very glad I was warned about it. I like the fact that there's no gun culture here, but I don't necessarily feel safer. There's a frisson in London that's similar to Los Angeles or New York, a sense that something might happen at any moment, and I really appreciate that. If I was moving for safety's sake, I'd head for somewhere like Vancouver, but I enjoy living in a country that's a bit raw. In America, there's a real sense of danger right now, a sense that lightning might strike at any time; it's not attractive. I prefer the edginess I find in London.

'Even given a few concerns about safety, this is a great place for kids to grow up. I have two, and I'd like them to have as much exposure as possible to Britain and to Europe. It's a culture you carry with you throughout your life, and it gives you an appreciation for the more intellectual side of life. In London, my kids experience a sense of history that's impossible to find in California. Walking along any street, you can feel the history practically saturating the pavement. Maybe you'd feel a hint of that in LA if anyone ever walked, but they don't. Everybody drives, and that gives the place a very different feel. You end up spending a lot more time by yourself in this hermetically sealed environment, rather than being out of the streets, meeting people.

'Here the traffic seems much more haphazard. I can understand why people bitch about it. It's incredibly crowded and sometimes impossible to get anywhere fast. I was taking a cab to the theatre today, we got stuck along the way, and I had to get out and run. When I have time to cruise around town, I tend to opt for rickshaws. It's a fine way to travel. Although I've lived in LA for a long while, my childhood was spent in New York, and I think that makes adapting to British life a little easier. Growing up, I was fascinated by the New York theatre. There's a similar culture here and an appreciation for the higher things in life. One of the differences that I've noticed, though, is that there seems to be a much younger audience here than in New York. The theatre seems much more accessible, both financially and culturally.

'Another consequence of coming from New York is that there's less temptation to bitch about the British weather, and if anything I think London's a little warmer. That said, I do sometimes miss the LA sunshine. What I really like about London is the authenticity here. That applies to people as much as the culture. I've seen some very well put-together British women, don't get me wrong, but generally the women here seem to be more upfront and authentic than they do in LA. There, any natural beauty, physical or otherwise, tends to get muddied over with a certain gloss.'

Christian won rave reviews and a Theatregoers' Choice Best Actor award for his performance in *One Flew Over the Cuckoo's Nest*, and he enjoyed the experience so much that, on his return to America, he headed straight for Broadway to join Jessica Lange and Sarah Paulson in a production of Tennessee Williams's *The Glass Menagerie*. According to the review in *The Advocate*, the play ranked alongside Arthur Miller's *Death of a Salesman* and Eugene O'Neill's *Long Day's Journey Into Night* in the pantheon of classic American dramas that crystallise the love and sadness, dreams and desperation, that haunt family life. 'Nakedly autobiographical,' the review ran, 'the play is narrated by Tom Wingfield (Christian Slater), a would-be writer chafing in a dead-end job and itching to fly the coop like his father did, leaving his crippled and depressed older sister, Laura (Paulson), in the care of their frustrated, overbearing mother, Amanda (Lange).

'In the tepid Broadway revival awkwardly staged by David Leveaux, none of the actors is especially well cast, though Lange pulls off the second act's climactic scene. Having wheedled Tom into bringing home from the factory a friend (Josh Lucas) as a potential date for Laura, Amanda turns the arrival of the gentleman caller into a referendum on her own attractiveness. Quivering with nervous vanity and unconscious destructiveness, Lange intriguingly conjures parallels between Amanda Wingfield and Williams's most famous beautiful dreamer, Blanche DuBois.'

Even during the play's run to July 2005 at the Ethel Barrymore Theater, Christian was thinking about his plans to return to the West End to star in another Tennessee Williams play, *Sweet Bird of Youth*, about an aging movie star and a gigolo. The play had originally been written for Elizabeth Taylor, yet Geraldine Page landed the role on Broadway and in film years before Taylor finally starred in a television version at the age of fifty-seven.

Christian also reckoned that 'it might be cool to spend the next thirty-five years in London', not only to work but also, perhaps, to continue his offstage social life in drinking establishments, karaoke bars and appearing on the town with a number of different women. As one insider confirmed, 'Christian has always had a wild streak. He is like a big kid who doesn't know when the party is over, and London is like a giant playground for him. Here, he's a big movie star and he has enjoyed the attention, but Ryan wants a stable family life for her children and, as much as he tries to fulfil the role of a good father and husband, Christian is finding it hard to leave his wild drinking days behind. Going out for a drink with him is like a marathon pub-crawl. He gets loud and boisterous; he loves attractive women and will just start talking to them. Sometimes he gets on a table and sings.'

According to the same source who spoke to the *Mail on Sunday*, his marriage reached a crisis point when Ryan learned of Christian's close friendship with a fashion assistant. 'They had a furious row and she threw him out of the house they had rented in west London. She has always stood by him, but this was the last straw. She put on a brave front and attended his final performance, but she is furious and has threatened to take the children back to the States.' She did.

Rumours of Christian's offstage behaviour in Britain quickly began to circulate even before the play hit the West End. In Scotland, where it opened at the Edinburgh Fringe in August 2004, he instantly started to make waves. 'Christian was put up in a flat in Leith,' said one of the festival organisers, 'but … he moved into the Sheraton Hotel.' Soon after he moved in, others guests noticed instances of noise and exuberant behaviour. The trouble, it seemed, was that Christian would keep inviting friends back to his hotel room. He was hanging about with an American guy called Dave Stone – a guy he met in rehab – and they had a lot of fun together, going out drinking regularly. 'They always started the evening drinking cocktails at the private Hallion Club and then they might go to a seedy pub and play snooker,' reported the Festival organiser. 'One night, it was alleged Christian got very drunk he was asked to leave the bar at the Assembly Rooms.

On another evening at the Festival, Christian turned up to a sold-out burlesque show featuring an erotic strip routine. He asked for a table at the front, near the stage, only to decide ten minutes later that he wanted to leave, which caused a little disruption.

One former colleague says, 'He sees London as a big candy store and has been busy stuffing himself. What he likes most is to drink and party. When he's not in a bar, he's out at a club. He says it's his way of unwinding. But, by all accounts, it is London's edge that appeals to him most.'

During his run in *One Flew Over the Cuckoo's Nest*, observers noted that Christian could sometimes be found in such private members' bars as Soho House and the Century

Club. 'He came in quite often,' said a former barman at the Century. 'He usually had other members of the cast with him. He's a pretty friendly guy.' Christian apparently often paid for private parties at the club so that he and his friends could party together.

All of these activities, it is claimed, took place while Ryan was still in America. Now it appears that Ryan has finally reached the end of her tether with this charming but complex character who seems firmly stuck in the hedonistic days of the late '80s and early '90s, when he was one of the young lions of Hollywood's Generation X. That was the era in which Slater – professionally, at least – could do no wrong, and by the time he appeared on stage at the West End he had starred in more than thirty films, but privately his life was spinning out of control. 'I had fame at an early age,' he said recently, 'and, yeah, that opened doors, but it was also confusing and frightening. I didn't really know who I was at that time. I didn't have a clear grasp on my personality.' Perhaps that's not surprising for someone whose entire life has been acting.

As one would expect, his mother, Mary Jo, still runs to his defence any time there is sign of trouble. The *Seattle Post* noted how she is still treating him like a baby bear after she apparently blasted a columnist working for New York's *Daily News* who suggested he was seeing teen star Lindsay Lohan, seventeen years younger than Christian. Certainly, had the rumours been true of her and Christian's relationship, it would have been a match made in tabloid heaven – and, if it wasn't, who could blame Mary Jo for wanting only nice things printed about her son? 'Christian has many wonderful traits,' she affirmed. 'He made mistakes. He was young and wild. Perhaps Lindsay can benefit from Christian's experience.'

Of course, some observers have even suggested Christian's reputation makes him a bad risk for the West End, although *One Flew Over the Cuckoo's Nest* producer, Nica Burns, disagrees. 'Apart from the few days when chicken pox delayed the show's opening, he was there every night for seventeen weeks. People expect him to be this mad person, but he really is a sweetie who loves life and tries to enjoy all that it has to offer.'

Maybe that's true, but at the same time, with an impressive career in film, television and on the stage, no matter what anyone might have been shouting from the top of the Hollywood Hills or from some dingy corner in London's West End, Christian Slater has established himself as one of the most talented and respected actors of his generation. As Winona Ryder said in 1989, 'He's one of the funniest people I know. He has a style that's really his own. Forty years from now someone is going to write a book called *Slater: The Legend*.' And, although slightly earlier than Ryder had predicted, and with a different title, this book is testimony to her foresight.

It would also be correct to conclude that, over the last ten years, Christian has become the embodiment of teenage cool, and that is probably what he will always best be known for. As film critic James Cameron-Wilson once noted, although he wasn't particularly handsome, like, say, Luke Perry, wasn't wildly athletic like Patrick Swayze, didn't mumble in the tradition of Matt Dillon, wasn't as notorious as, say, Rob Lowe, and even if he wasn't as good an actor as Sean Penn or Eric Stoltz, he *did* have attitude. And that, in the 1990s, counted for a hell of a lot.

Filmography

The Legend of Billie Jean (1985)
Directed by Matthew Robbins. Screenplay by
Walter Bernstein, Lawrence Konner and Mark Rosenthal.
Released by Tristar Pictures.
Cast: Helen Slater, Keith Gordon, Christian Slater,
Richard Bradford, Peter Coyote, Martha Gehman,
Yeardley Smith, Dean Stockwell, Barry Tubb.

The Name of the Rose (1986)
Directed by Jean-Jacques Annaud. Screenplay by Umberto
Eco, Andrew Birkin, Gerard Brach, Howard Franklin and
Alain Godard. Released by Twentieth Century-Fox.
Cast: Sean Connery, F Murray Abraham, Christian Slater,
Elva Baskin, Michael Lonsdale, Volker Prechtel,
Feodor Chaliapin Jnr, William Hickey, Michael Habeck,
Ron Perlman.

Twisted (1986)

Directed by Adam Holender. Screenplay by Glenn Kershaw and Bruce Graham, based on the play by Jack Horrigan. Released by Hemdale Film Corporation.
Cast: Lois Smith, Christian Slater, Dina Merrill, Tandy Cronyn, Dan Ziskie, Brooke Tracey, John Cunningham, Edward Marshall, Laurie Kennedy, JC Quinn.

Tucker: The Man and his Dream (1988)

Directed by Francis Ford Coppola. Screenplay by Arnold Schulman and David Seidler. Released by Paramount Pictures.
Cast: Jeff Bridges, Joan Allen, Martin Landau, Frederic Forrest, Mako, Elias Kopteas, Christian Slater, Niona Siemaszko, Anders Johnson, Corin Nemec, Marshall Bell.

Gleaming the Cube (1989)

Directed by Graeme Clifford. Screenplay by Michael Tolkin. Released by Twentieth Century-Fox.
Cast: Christian Slater, Steven Bauer, Richard Herd, Le Taun, Min Luong, Art Chiudabala, Ed Lauter, Micole Mercurio, Peter Kwong, Charles Cyphers, Max Perlich, Tony Hawk, Tommy Guerrero, Christian Jacobs.

Heathers (1989)

Directed by Michael Lehmann. Screenplay by Daniel Waters. Released by New World Pictures.
Cast: Winona Ryder, Christian Slater, Shannen Doherty, Kim Walker, Lisanne Falk, Penelope Milford, Glenn Shadix, Lance Fenton, Patrick Labyorteaux.

Beyond the Stars (1989)
Directed and written by David Saperstein. Released by
Moviestore Entertainment.
Cast: Martin Sheen, Christian Slater, Robert Foxworth,
Sharon Stone, Olivia d'Abo, F Murray Abraham, Don S Davis,
William S Taylor, Babs Chula, Terence Kelly, Freda Perry,
Campbell Lane, Robert Benedetti, Christine Anton.

The Wizard (1989)
Directed by Todd Holland. Screenplay by David Chisholm.
Released by Universal Pictures.
Cast: Luke Edwards, Vince Trankina, Wendy Phillips,
Dea McAllister, Sam McMurray, Beau Bridges, Fred Savage,
Christian Slater, Will Seltzer, Roy Conrad, Jenny Lewis,
Roderick Dexter.

Tales from the Darkside: The Movie (1990)
Directed by John Harrison. Screenplay by
Michael McDowell, based on a story by Sir Arthur Conan
Doyle. Released by Paramount Pictures.
Cast: Deborah Harry, David Forrester, Matthew Lawrence,
Christian Slater, Robert Sedgwick, Steve Buscemi,
Donald Van Horn, Michael Deak, Julianne Moore.

Young Guns II (1990)
Directed by Geoff Murphy. Screenplay by John Fusco.
Released by Twentieth Century-Fox.
Cast: Emilio Estevez, Kiefer Sutherland, Lou Diamond
Phillips, Christian Slater, William L Petersen, Alan Ruck,
RD Call, James Coburn, Balthazar Getty, Jack Kehoe,

Robert Knepper, Tom Kurlander, Viggo Mortensen,
Leon Rippy.

Pump Up the Volume (1990)
Directed and written by Allan Moyle. Released by
New Line Cinema.
Cast: Christian Slater, Andy Romano, Keith Stuart Thayer,
Cheryl Pollak, Jeff Chamberlain, Billy Morrissette,
Samantha Mathis, Lala Stolman, Holly Sampson, Annie Ross,
Anthony Lucero, Annie Rusoff, Jonathan Mazer.

Robin Hood: Prince of Thieves (1991)
Directed by Kevin Reynolds. Screenplay by Pen Densham
and John Watson. Released by Warner Brothers.
Cast: Kevin Costner, Morgan Freeman, Mary Elizabeth
Mastrantonio, Christian Slater, Alan Rickman,
Geraldine McEwan, Michael McShane, Brian Blessed,
Michael Wincott, Nick Brimble, Soo Drouet,
Daniel Newman, Daniel Peacock, Walter Sparrow.

Mobsters (1991)
Directed by Michael Karbelnikoff. Screenplay by
Michael Mahern. Released by Universal Pictures.
Cast: Christian Slater, Patrick Dempsey, Richard Grieco,
Costas Mandylor, F Murray Abraham, Lara Flynn Boyle,
Michael Gambon, Chris Penn, Anthony Quinn,
Rodney Eastman, Jeremy Schoenberg, Miles Perlich.

Star Trek VI: The Undiscovered Country (1991)
Directed by Nicholas Myers. Screenplay by Nicholas Myers
and Denny Martin Flinn. Released by Paramount Pictures.
Cast: William Shatner, Leonard Nimoy, DeForest Kelley,
James Doohan, Walter Koenig, Nichelle Nichols,
George Takei, Kim Cattrall, Mark Lenard, Grace Lee
Whitney, Christian Slater.

Kuffs (1992)
Directed by Bruce A Evans. Screenplay by Bruce A Evans
and Raynold Gideon. Released by Universal Pictures.
Cast: Christian Slater, Milla Jovovich, Ric Roman Waugh,
Steve Holladay, Chad Randall, Clarke Coleman,
Leon Rippy, Craig Benton, Ashley Judd, Bruce Boxleitner,
Joshua Cadman, Mary Ellen Trainor.

FernGully: The Last Rainforest (1992)
Directed by Bill Croyer. Screenplay by Jim Cox and
Diana Young. Released by Twentieth Century-Fox.
Voice cast: Tim Curry, Samantha Mathis, Christian Slater,
Jonathan Ward, Robin Williams, Grace Zabriskie,
Geoffrey Blake, Robert Pastorelli, Cheech Marin,
Tommy Chong, Tone Loc, Townsend Coleman,
Brian Cummings.

Where the Day Takes You (1992)
Directed by Marc Rocco. Screenplay by Michael
Hitchcock, Marc Rocco and Kurt Voss. Released by
New Line Cinema.
Cast: Laura San Giacomo, Dermot Mulroney,

Robert Knepper, Sean Astin, Balthazar Getty, Will Smith,
James LeGros, Ricki Lake, Lara Flynn Boyle, Peter Dobson,
MacLachlan, Adam Baldwin, Christian Slater (uncredited).

Untamed Heart (1993)
Directed by Tony Bill. Screenplay by Tom Sierchio.
Released by United International Pictures (UIP).
Cast: Christian Slater, Marisa Tomei, Rosie Perez,
Kyle Secor, Willie Garson, James Cada, Gary Groomes,
Claudia Wilkens, Pat Clemons, Lotis Key, Vanessa Hart,
Charley Bartlett.

True Romance (1993)
Directed by Tony Scott. Screenplay by Quentin Tarantino.
Released by Warner Brothers.
Cast: Christian Slater, Patricia Arquette, Dennis Hopper,
Val Kilmer, Gary Oldman, Brad Pitt, Christopher Walken,
Bronson Pinchot, Samuel L Jackson, Michael Rapport,
Saul Rubinek, Conchata Ferrell, James Gandolfini,
Anna Levine.

Jimmy Hollywood (1994)
Directed and written by Barry Levinson. Released by
Paramount Pictures.
Cast: Joe Pesci, Christian Slater, Victoria Abril, Jason Beghe,
John Cothran Jr, Hal Fishman, Jerry Dunphy,
Andrea Kutyas, Kerry Kilbridge, Paula Lopez, Paul Dean
Jackson, Joe Avellar, Susan Campos.

Interview with the Vampire: The Vampire Chronicles (1994)
Directed by Neil Jordan. Screenplay by Anne Rice.
Released by Warner Brothers.
Cast: Tom Cruise, Brad Pitt, Kirsten Dunst, Stephen Rea,
Antonio Banderas, Christian Slater, Virginia McCollam,
John McConnell, Mike Seelig, Bellina Logan,
Thandie Newton, Indra Ove, Helen McCrory.

Murder in the First (1995)
Directed by Marc Rocco. Screenplay by Dan Gordon.
Released by Warner Brothers.
Cast: Christian Slater, Kevin Bacon, Gary Oldman,
Embeth Davidtz, William H Macy, Stephen Tobolowsky,
Brad Dourif, R Lee Ermey, Mia Kirshner, Ben Slack.

Bed of Roses (1996)
Directed and written by Michael Goldenberg. Released by
New Line Cinema.
Cast: Christian Slater, Mary Stuart Masterson, Pamela Segall,
Josh Brolin, Brian Tarantina, Debra Monk, Mary Alice,
Kenneth Cranham, Ally Walker, Anne Pitoniak,
Michael Haley.

Broken Arrow (1996)
Directed by John Woo. Screenplay by Graham Yost.
Released by Twentieth Century-Fox.
Cast: John Travolta, Christian Slater, Samantha Mathis,
Delroy Lindo, Bob Gunton, Frank Whaley, Howie Long,
Vondie Curtis-Hall, Jack Thompson, Vyto Ruginis,
Ousaun Elam.

Austin Powers: International Man of Mystery (1997)
Directed by Jay Roach. Screenplay by Michael Myers.
Released by New Line Cinema.
Cast: Michael Myers, Elizabeth Hurley, Michael York,
Mimi Rogers, Robert Wagner, Seth Green, Fabina Udenio,
Mindy Sterling, Paul Dillon, Charles Napier, Will Ferrell,
Christian Slater (uncredited cameo).

Julian Po (1997)
Directed and written by Alan Wade. Released by
Fine Line Features.
Cast: Christian Slater, Robin Tunney, Michael Parks,
Cherry Jones, Frankie Faison, Harve Presnell, Allison Janney,
LaTanya Richardson, Dina Spybey, Bruce Bohne.

Hard Rain (1998)
Directed by Mikael Salomon. Screenplay by Graham Yost.
Released by Paramount Pictures.
Cast: Morgan Freeman, Christian Slater, Randy Quaid,
Minnie Driver, Edward Asner, Michael A Goorjian,
Dann Florek, Ricky Harris, Mark Rolston, Peter Murnick,
Wayne Duvall.

Basil (1998)
Directed and written by Radha Bharadwaj. Released by
Kushner–Locke Company.
Cast: Christian Slater, Jared Leto, Stephanie Bagsha,
Crispin Bonham-Carter, Jenny Downham, Claire Forlani,
Anne Louise Grimshaw, Sarah Hadland, Carli Harris,
Derek Jacobi, Joanna John, Georgiana Johnson, Jackson Leach.

Very Bad Things (1998)
Directed and written by Peter Berg. Released by
Polygram Filmed Entertainment.
Cast: Jon Favreau, Leland Orser, Cameron Diaz,
Christian Slater, Rob Brownstein, Jeremy Piven, Daniel Stern,
Jeanne Tripplehorn, Joey Zimmerman, Tyler Cole Malinger,
Kobe Tai, Russell B McKenzie.

Love Stinks (1999)
Directed and written by Jeff Franklin. Released by
Independent Artists.
Cast: French Stewart, Bridgette Wilson, Tyra Banks,
Steve Hytner, Jason Bateman, Tiffani Thiessen, Ellis Williams,
Ivana Milicevic, Christian Slater (uncredited cameo).

White Lies (1999)
Directed by Michael Adams. Screenplay by Michael Adams
and Donna Adams. Released by Nighthawk Pictures.
Cast: Franco Nero, Christian Slater.

The Contender (2000)
Directed and written by Rod Lurie. Released by
DreamWorks Distribution.
Cast: Gary Oldman, Joan Allen, Jeff Bridges, Christian Slater,
Sam Elliot, William L Petersen, Saul Rubinek, Philip Baker
Hall, Mike Binder, Robin Thomas.

3,000 Miles To Graceland (2000)
Directed by Demian Lichtenstein. Screenplay by Demian
Lichtenstein, Richard Recco and Eric Manes. Released by
Warner Brothers.
Cast: Kurt Russell, Kevin Costner, Courtney Cox,
Christian Slater, Kevin Pollack, David Arquette, Jon Lovitz,
Howie Long, Thomas Haden Church, Bokeem Woodbine,
Ice-T, David Kaye, Louis Lombardi, Shawn Michael Howard.

Who Is Cletis Tout? (2001)
Directed and written by Chris Ver Weil. Released by
Paramount Pictures.
Cast: Christian Slater, Tim Allen, Portia de Rossi,
Richard Dreyfuss, Billy Connolly, Peter MacNeill, Elias Zarou,
Richard Chevolleau, RuPaul, Joseph Scoren, Eugene Lipinski.

Zoolander (2001)
Directed by Ben Stiller. Screenplay by Drake Sather,
Ben Stiller and John Hamburg.
Released by Paramount Pictures.
Cast: Ben Stiller, Owen Wilson, Christine Taylor, Will Ferrell,
Milla Jovovich, Jerry Stiller, David Duchovny, Jon Voight,
Judah Friedlander, Nathan Lee Graham, Alexandre Manning,
Asio Highsmith, Alexander Skarsgard, Donald Trump,
Christian Slater, Winona Ryder (uncredited).

Run for the Money (also known as *Hard Cash*) (2002)
Directed by Predrag Antonijevic. Screenplay by
Willie Dreyfus. Released by Canyon Productions.
Cast: Christian Slater, Val Kilmer, Sara Downing,

Vincent Laresca, Balthazar Getty, Bokeem Woodbine,
Daryl Hannah, Rodney Rowland, Holliston Coleman,
Peter Woodward, Michael Anthony Rosas, William Forsythe.

Windtalkers (2002)
Directed by John Woo. Screenplay by John Rice and
Joe Batteer. Released by MGM.
Cast: Nicolas Cage, Adam Beach, Peter Stormare,
Noah Emmerich, Mark Ruffalo, Brian Van Holt,
Martin Henderson, Roger Willie, Frances O'Connor,
Christian Slater, Jason Isaacs, Billy Morts, Cameron Thor,
Kevin Cooney, Holmes Osborne.

Masked and Anonymous (2003)
Directed by Larry Charles. Screenplay by Bob Dylan and
Larry Charles. Released by Sony Pictures.
Cast: Bob Dylan, Jeff Bridges, Penelope Cruz, John
Goodman, Jessica Lange, Luke Wilson, Angela Bassett,
Steven Bauer, Bruce Dern, Michael Paul Chan, Ed Harris,
Val Kilmer, Chris Penn, Christian Slater.

Mindhunters (2004)
Directed by Renny Harlin. Screenplay by Wayne Kramer
and Kevin Brodbin. Released by Dimension Films.
Cast: Eion Bailey, Clifton Collins Jr, Will Kemp, Val Kilmer,
Johnny Lee Miller, Kathryn Morris, Christian Slater,
LL Cool J, Patrick Velasquez, Cassandra Bell.

Churchill: The Hollywood Years (2004)
Directed by Peter Richardson. Screenplay by
Peter Richardson and Pete Richens. Released by Pathé Films.
Cast: Neve Campbell, Christian Slater, Mark Caven,
Phil Cornwell, McKenzie Crook, Jon Culshaw, Simon Day,
James Dreyfus, Harry Enfield, Rik Mayall, Bob Mortimer,
Leslie Phillips, Vic Reeves, Steve Pemberton,
Miranda Richardson, Jessica Oyelowo, Antony Sher.

Pursued (2004)
Directed by Kristoffer Tabori. Screenplay by Peter M Lenkov.
Released by Artisan Entertainment.
Cast: Gill Belows, Conchita Campbell, Michael Clarke
Duncan, Chelah Horsdal, Christian Slater, Ken Tremblett,
Estella Warren.

The Deal (2004)
Directed by Harvey Kahn. Screenplay by Ruth Epstein.
Cast: Christian Slater, Selma Blair, John Heard,
Angie Harmon, Colm Feore, Robert Loggia, Francoise Yip,
Mike Dopud, Philip Granger.

The Good Shepherd (2004)
Directed by Lewin Webb. Screenplay by Brad Mirman.
Cast: Christian Slater, Molly Parker, Stephen Rea,
Gordon Pinsent, James Dallas Smith, Colin Glazer,
Duane Murray, Alex Paxton.

A Light Knight's Odyssey (2004)
Directed by Adrian Carr. Screenplay by Harry 'Doc' Kloor.
Produced by Jupiter 9 Productions.
Voice cast: Annie Archer, Lacey Chabert, Sarah Michelle
Gellar, Samuel L Jackson, James Earl Jones, Casey Kasem,
Jim Meskimem, Robert Picardo, Tait Ruppert,
Christian Slater, John Travolta, David Warner, Michael York.

Alone in the Dark (2005)
Directed by Uwe Boll. Screenplay by Elan Mastai,
Michael Roesch and Peter Scheerer. Released by
Lions Gate Films.
Cast: Christian Slater, Tara Reid, Stephen Dorff, Will
Sanderson, Mark Acheson, Ed Anders, Robert Bruce,
Daniel Cudmore, Mike Dopud, John Fallon, Karin Konoval,
Catherine Lough Haggquist, Ho Sung Pak, Malcolm Scott.

A License to Steal (2005)
Directed by Robert Greenhut. Screenplay by
Gregory Marquette.
Cast: Christian Slater, William Hurt, Michael Madsen,
Frankie Valli, Frank Vincent.

Theatre

The Music Man (City Centre Theater, New York, 1980)
Directed by Michael Kidd. Written by Meredith Wilson in
collaboration with Franklin Lacey.
Cast: Dick Van Dyke, Meg Bussert, Iggie Wolfington,
Victoria Ally, Alis-Eaine Anderson, Carol Arthur,

Carol Ann Busch, Dennis Batutis, David Beckett, Ralph Braun, Marcia Brushingham, Larry Cahn, Mark A Esposito, Mary Gaebler, Tom Garrett, Liza Gennaro, Dennis Holland, Andy Hostettler, Tony Jaeqer, JJ Jepson, Jen Jones, Wendy Kimball, Ara Marx, Calvin McRae, Darleigh Miller, Lara Jill Miller, Randy Morgan, PJ Nelson, Gail Pennigton, Richard Wareen Pugh, Rosemary Rado, Mary Roche, Michael J Rockne, Christian Slater, Coley Sohn, Jay Stuart, Peter Wandal, Lee Winston.

Copperfield (ANTA Theater, New York, 1981)
Directed by Rob Iscove. Written by Al Kasha and
Joel Hirschhorn. Based on the book *David Copperfield* by
Charles Dickens.
Cast: David Ray Bartee, Ralph Braun, Katharine Buffaloe,
Maris Clement, Michael Connolly, Michael Danek,
Daniel Dee, Leslie Denniston, Spence Ford, Beulah Garrick,
Heather Lee Gerdes, Michael Gorman, David Horwitz,
Barrie Ingham, George S Irving, Mary Mastrantonio,
Carmen Mathews, Brian Matthews, Pamela McLernon,
Darleigh Miller, Dana Moore, Gary Munch, Keith Perry,
Linda Poser, Richard Warren Pugh, Brian Quinn,
Evan Richards, Lynn Savage, Bruce Sherman, Christian
Slater, Mary Stout, Claude Tessier, Missy Whitchurch,
Lenny Wolpe.

Macbeth (Circle in the Square Theater, New York, 1982)
Directed by Nicol Williamson. Written by
William Shakespeare.
Cast: Rand Bridges, Elaine Bromka, Renato Cibelli,

Rik Colitti, John Henry Cox, Ray Dooley, Paul Falzone,
Joyce Fideor, Bette Henritze, Mark Herrier, Peter James,
Richard Jamieson, Neal Jones, Tara Loewenstern,
Tom McDermott, Peter McRobbie, Gregory Mortensen,
Paul Perri, Peter Phillips, Christian Slater, JT Walsh,
Andrea Weber, Nicol Williamson, John Woida.

Merlin (Mark Hellinger Theater, New York, 1983)
Directed by Ivan Reitman. Written by Richard Levinson
and William Link.
Cast: Doug Henning, Chita Rivera, George Lee Andrews,
David Asher, Alan Brasington, Robin Cleaver, Spence Ford,
Ramon Galindo, Pat Gorman, Andrea Handler,
Debbie Henning, Leslie Hicks, Nathan Lane, Sandy Laufer,
Robyn Lee, Todd Lester, Joe Locarro, Edmund Lyndeck,
Fred C Mann III, Gregory Mitchell, Andrew Hill Newman,
Michelle Nicastro, Peggy Parten, Iris Revson, Claudia Shell,
Christian Slater, Robert Tanna, Robert Warners,
Rebecca Wright.

Side Man (John Golden Theater, New York, 1999)
Directed by Michael Mayer. Written by Warren Leight.
Cast: Eddie Falco, Marissa Matrone, Andrew McCarthy,
Michael O'Keefe, Robert Sella, Christian Slater,
Angelica Torn, Scott Wolf.

One Flew Over the Cuckoo's Nest (The Assembly Rooms,
Edinburgh, 2004, and Gielgud Theatre, London, 2004/5)
Directed by Terry Johnson and Tamara Harvey. Written by
Dale Wasserman. Based on the novel by Ken Kesey.

Cast: Christian Slater, McKenzie Crook, Francis Barber,
Tim Ahern, Stephen K Amos, Ian Coppinger,
Brendan Dempsey, Felix Dexter, Katherine Jakeway,
Dave John, Phil Nichol, Owen O'Neill, Lucy Porter,
Gavin Robertson, Lizzie Roper.

The Glass Menagerie (Ethel Barrymore Theater,
New York, 2005)
Directed by David Leveaux. Written by Tennessee Williams.
Cast: Jessica Lange, Josh Lucas, Sarah Paulson, Christian Slater.

Television

Sherlock Holmes (TV movie, 1981)
Directed by Peter H Hunt. Screenplay by William Gillette.
Produced by and for HBO.
Cast: Frank Langella, Susan Clark, Stephen Collins,
Richard Woods, George Morfogen, Laurie Kennedy,
Tom Atkins, Louis Beachner, Robert Brolli, William Duell,
Jennifer Harmon, Sebastian Moran, Michael Quill,
Christian Slater, Ralph Strait, John Tillinger, Barbara Tweed.

Living Proof: The Hank Williams Jr Story (TV movie, 1983)
Directed by Dick Lowry. Screenplay by Stephen Candel
and IC Rapoport. Based on the book *Living Proof* by Hank
Williams Jr and Michael Bane. Produced by and for NBC.
Cast: Richard Thomas, Lenora May, Liane Langland,
Ann Gillespie, Merle Kilgore, Clu Gulager, Allyn Ann
McLerie, Barton Heyman, Noble Willingham, Jay O Sanders,

Christian Slater, Jonathan Hogan, Mickey Jones,
Naomi Judd, Connie Freeman.

The Haunted Mansion Mystery (TV movie, 1983)
Directed by Larry Elikann. Screenplay by Rod Baker and
Glen Olson. Based on the novel by Virginia Masterman-
Smith. Produced by Scholastic Productions for
ABC Network.
Cast: Tristine Skyler, Christian Slater, Cheryl Giannini,
Paul Hecht, Thomas Barbour, Jonathan Ward,
Jimmie Ray Weeks, Olivia Laurel Mates, Matthew Kolmes.

Ryan's Hope (TV series, 1975–89)
Series created by Paul Aliva Mayer and Claire Labine.
Screenplay by various writers.
Produced for ABC Television. Cast: various, including
Christian Slater (1985).

Secrets (TV movie, 1986)
Directed by Fred Barzyk. Screenplay by Laura Harrington.
Produced by Lisa Schmid.
Cast: Debbie Bancroft, ML Carr, Jon DeVries,
Barbara Feldon, Christian Slater.

Desperate for Love (TV movie, 1989)
Directed by Michael Tuchner. Screenplay by Judith Paige
Mitchell. Produced by and for Lorimar Television.
Cast: Christian Slater, Tammy Lauren, Brian Bloom,
Veronica Cartwright, Scott Paulin, Arthur Rosenberg,
Amy O'Neill, Lulee Fisher, Michael Flynn, Billy Vera,

David Dwyer, Rebecca Wackler, Peter Thomasson, Keith Noble.

Merry Christmas, George Bailey (1997)
Directed by Matthew Diamond. Produced for and by Public Broadcasting Service.
Cast: Casey Kasem, Bill Pullman, Penelope Ann Miller, Nathan Lane, Martin Landau, Sally Field, Joe Mantegna, Christian Slater, Jerry Van Dyke, Robert Guillaume, Carol Kane, Bronson Pinchot, Dan Lauria, Craig Sheffer, Armelia McQueen.

Prehistoric Planet (TV series, 2002)
Written by David Bock and Peter Sherman. Narrators: Ben Stiller, Christian Slater.

Producer

Hard Rain (co-producer, 1998)
Basil (co-producer, 1998)
Very Bad Things (executive producer, 1998)
The Deal (executive producer, 2004)

Director

Museum of Love (1996)

Awards and Nominations

Independent Spirit Awards

1991
Pump Up the Volume
(nominated for Best Male Performance)

MTV Movie Awards

1992
Kuffs
(nominated for Most Desirable Male)

1993
Untamed Heart
(nominated for Best Kiss with Marisa Tomei; won for
Most Desirable Male)

1994
True Romance
(nominated for Best Kiss with Patricia Arquette)

1995
Interview with the Vampire: The Vampire Chronicles
(nominated for Most Desirable Male)

1996
Broken Arrow
(nominated for Best Fight with John Travolta)

Csapnivaló Golden Slate Awards

2000
Very Bad Things
(won Best Male Performance)

Broadcast Film Critics' Association Alan J Pakula Award

2001
The Contender
(won Artistic Excellence, with other cast members)

Theatregoers' Choice Theatre Award

2005
One Flew Over the Cuckoo's Nest
(won Best Actor in a Play)